HIDDEN FERMANAGH

Traditional Music and Song from County Fermanagh

Cyril Maguire

Transcriptions by
Sharon Creasey

Fermanagh Traditional Music Society

First published in 2003 by
The Fermanagh Traditional Music Society
Drumbeggan
Monea
County Fermanagh
Northern Ireland

© The Fermanagh Traditional Music Society, 2003

All rights reserved. No part of this book may be reprinted or reproduced or utilised in any electronic, mechanical or other means, now known or hereafter invented, including photocopying and recording or otherwise, without either the prior written permission of the Publishers or a licence permitting restricted copying in Ireland issued by the Irish Copyright Licensing Agency Ltd, The Irish Writers' Centre, 19 Parnell Square, Dublin 1.

The author has asserted his moral rights in this work.

British Library Cataloguing in Publication Data
A CIP catalogue record for this book is available from the British Library

ISBN 0-9546200-0-3

Typeset by Guildhall Press, Derry
Printed by Colour Books, Dublin

Website Address: www.fermanaghmusic.com

Acknowledgements

My thanks to all those people from Fermanagh who so freely gave of their time and talents.

CONTENTS

FOREWORD		vi
INTRODUCTION		1
CHAPTER 1	A Life in Music	3
CHAPTER 2	The Gunn Book	23
CHAPTER 3	A Life on Stage	33
CHAPTER 4	Song and Verse	51
DANCE MUSIC AND SONGS		71
BIBLIOGRAPHY		168
INDEX OF DANCE MUSIC		170
INDEX OF SONGS		171

FOREWORD

Hide – conceal from sight intentionally or not
Concise Oxford Dictionary

I have met some people who would hide traditional music and song to maintain its purity. Today, they would rarely admit to this attitude and it is one with which I have never agreed and it is certainly on the wane.

Something is also in a sense *hidden* when you have no interest in it. Thus those who feel that way may define this music as *specialist,* though those of us who are involved see that as diminishing the music, often through lack of knowledge.

In the late '50s and the early '60s, many of us thought traditional music and song were in terminal decline, especially in the Six Counties. Little was broadcast on radio or TV, few recordings were available and concerts were rare. The music was *hidden* by the neglect of the establishment.

In 1964, I returned from studying in London, fired with the desire to search out and collect as many of these old songs as possible before they disappeared completely. My discovery of a *hidden* Armagh was through my farmer uncle, Tom McCreery. He introduced me to the singers of old songs and they, in turn, led me to others. At the same time, I met other searchers like myself who were entranced by the music that we had found (or which had found us). With youthful enthusiasm, we approached the Ulster Folk Museum, whose main interest seemed to be in saving and relocating physical artefacts like spade mills and village halls. We hoped they would make a good-quality tape recorder available for lending to collectors. We were told that we did not have the required qualifications. Amazed and disgusted, we carried on without their support. By the time they were doing anything really practical, many of us had been working in the field for years.

There were different responses to what we were finding. Some wished to study the material on an academic basis. Others simply wanted to perform and share this music. Most of us lay in between – fascinated by the folklore, themes, social history or musicology, but also performing for our own pleasure and that of others.

Fermanagh was a *hidden* world for me, the door to which was opened by the late Henry O'Prey, who, in about 1965, introduced me to Tommy (Jason) Gunn – fiddler, singer, dancer, bones player and telephone linesman, originally from Derrylin, County Fermanagh, by then presiding over a renowned céilidhe house in Botanic Avenue, Belfast.

A few of us, including John Moulden, Dave Scott and Terry Brown, formed the grandly-named Ulster Folk Music Society. We asked Tommy to perform there. And so the process began. He introduced us to other musicians such as Sean McAloon, the great piper from Roslea, James McMahon, fllute player, also Roslea, and John Rea, dulcimer player from the Glens of Antrim, Tom Ginley and so on. Tommy was also generous and lavish in his praise for a flute and whistle player from Bellanaleck. He suggested we bring him up to play at a concert in the city, and he wasn't wrong about Cathal McConnell. More doors opened as we became friends.

At Cathal's home in Bellanaleck, you met musicians who had arrived, often unannounced, from all over the place to sit and crack with Sandy and Mrs McConnell, to drink tea, play tunes, more talk, more tea, more music... Travelling around with Cathal, I had the privilege to meet most of the musicians you will find between these covers.

At the same time, other doors were opening. I had become friends with Paddy McMahon, brother of James, tunemaker and player of the ivory flute. I often visited him in his small house off Ormeau Avenue in Belfast, where we talked, and he sang me some fine songs. He told me he knew a great singer from his home place, Roslea. We went down and I met John (Jock) Maguire. John, in turn, introduced me to other singers... his brother and sister and his neighbours, Peter and Elly Mullarkey, and told me how, as a young man, he had crept up behind the turf stacks to hear and learn songs from Sean McAloon's father, who wouldn't perform in public, but had great songs and sang them while he cut turf. I was able to play my part in the process and return the compliment by introducing Cathal to John Maguire, and you'll find some of the songs carried by this great Roslea singer (indeed, one of Ireland's great singers) in this volume.

And so it goes on. Doors opening lead to more doors. The wheel keeps going round. These CDs and book continue this process. I hope you, the reader and listener, will be encouraged to go and open doors of your own.

There is a whole vigorous living tradition out there that is *hidden* because it is running paralled to what is served up to us as culture. But remember, when you find it, share and share alike, as the generous explorers who put together these CDs and book did. And so the tradition lives on and you will have played your part.

Robin Morton
Temple, 2003

Some members of the Fermanagh Traditional Music Society in The Ballyhugh Arts Centre. Left to right, standing: Pat McManus, Sharon Creasey, Cyril Maguire, Francis Rasdale, Valerie McManus, Mick Shannon. Left to right, seated: Cathal McConnell, Annie McKenzie, John McManus, Eileen McGourty, Fintan McManus, Mickey McConnell. Courtesy of Brian Mulligan, photographer, County Cavan.

INTRODUCTION
Hidden Fermanagh – The Project

The idea for this project came originally from Cathal McConnell. He mentioned to me, in late 2001, that he would like to put together a CD of Fermanagh music that had never before been recorded. I knew it would be possible to do this, as, down the years, Cathal had put a large number of Fermanagh tunes on tape for me, mostly those of Eddie Duffy and Mick Hoy. He was also anxious to include the material of John McManus, as John had always been his main source in his home part of the county. From the start, therefore, the project came to focus on two parts of the county: Derrylin and Derrygonnelly and their surrounding areas. It was the availability of so much material, in these two areas alone, that made this narrow focus possible.

We were also aware of the existence of *The Gunn Book*, a manuscript of tunes in the possession of the Gunn family, and of John McManus' connection to this manuscript (see Ch. 2). We had never seen it and knew nothing about it apart from its existence. John McManus arranged for me to see it, and its value was obvious, even from a brief inspection. It became an important source for us. We have, therefore, relied on three main sources: Cathal McConnell; John McManus and *The Gunn Book*.

To carry out the project, a number of us formed the Fermanagh Traditional Music Society and proceeded with Arts Council funding. The resulting recordings feature many singers and players who come mostly from the areas mentioned (we strayed a little bit, inevitably, but not very much). Gabriel McArdle is originally from close to Derrylin and has collected songs from there. Jim McGrath and Francis Rasdale come from the Derrygonnelly area, Monea and Boho respectively. Brenda McCann lives in Irvinestown, but her mother, Ann, is from Boho, and her grandfather played tin whistle and sang. She has always been familiar with the music in this part of the county.

Cathal McConnell holds a key position in all this; he is the link between the areas mentioned and has known all the people involved. He was the first person, many years ago, to recognise the importance of the Eddie Duffy and Mick Hoy repertoires. He is also a leading singer in the Northern style and has retained his early collections of Fermanagh songs. Accordingly, he was invited to be producer of the CDs.

Cyril Maguire

CHAPTER 1
A Life in Music

John and Valerie head the famous McManus music family from Knockninny, on the shores of Upper Lough Erne and close to Derrylin. Knockninny Hill, named after one of Fermanagh's best-known saints, Naomh Ninneadh, dominates the area and gives it its name. John and Valerie live in John's family home (their children are the seventh generation to live there) close to the shore of the lake and to Knockninny pier in the townland of Aughakillymaud (pronounced "Achlemad" locally). Music has been in John's family for many generations and he can trace this directly back to his great-great-grandfather, John Gunn, who also played fiddle and compiled *The Gunn Book*. Tommy, also known as Jason, Gunn, who became prominent in Belfast traditional circles and was the first fiddle player with The Boys of the Lough, was his cousin.

However, John's direct musical influence came from his mother, Katie Gunn, and his uncle, Hugh Gunn – brother and sister. Hugh played fiddle and Katie lilted and sang. They played together for house dances, more often referred to as "sprees" by John and Valerie. John began to play with them while still very young and this was the beginning of a lifelong involvement in music. He was naturally gifted with a wonderful memory (his recall was immediate), but his life story in music is characterised by great

Pat McManus with parents Valerie and John.

John McManus.

inventiveness and initiative. He led The Starlight Dance Band from 1942 until 1962 and was, at the same time, a member of the local Harp of Erin Céilidhe Band, so most of his public playing (and he was in constant demand locally for house dances or sprees of one kind or another) was done in what many now consider to have been a bleak time for traditional music, the 1940s and '50s. John's story doesn't confirm or contradict this – playing was part of their livelihood and they enjoyed it – but it does highlight how different things were back then. The radio was important but limited. The very convenient, portable cassette tape recorder was not available. Music and musical instruments were not so readily available. Travel was obviously more difficult and the performing circuit for musicians much smaller. There were "sessions", but not as we understand them now. John's story explains how at least one musician operated in this context.

Conversation with John and Valerie McManus, 15 February 2003.

Do you remember you were saying about being born in America?

John: Yes, I was six and a half when I left it. You see, well I suppose it all started... this is my father's place you see and there's seven generations... Pat[1] and all of them will be the seventh generation of us to have lived here in the same place, not another family in it. That's as far back as I could trace. Anyway, my father used to see this little lassie going up the road; she was Katie Gunn. Now, she was twelve years younger than him and he says, 'Now, there's the little girl I'm going to marry.' She crossed the road and there was a spring well out the field and she was going for water. It was then, in 1910, my father went to America. And... well, he was, what you might say, a hobo. He hadn't a penny to crash off one and other. He jumped trains and went to the lumber camps and eventually went out to a ranch in Wyoming and stayed there for a good many years. My mother then, in the meantime, had come to America (to her sister), and her sister wrote to my father saying that Katie had come to America. So he left Wyoming and came to New York and came to my Aunt Maggie's place and Katie was there. They chatted a while anyway and, 'Katie,' he says, 'it's time we were going down to the City Hall.' My mother says, 'What are we going down to the City Hall for?' 'To get a marriage licence,' says he. And this was the proposal, where it all started off. So, some months after, I was the first and the only one.

And she was Katie Gunn?

John: That's right.

And is that where your tune came from, the Katie's Lilt *that you play?*

John: That's right.

You were the only one to carry on the music?

John: That's right. You see, in her family there was seven brothers and seven sisters and ten of them played the fiddle. Well, they got married and of course there was a mess of children from them. But not one of them, of their children, carried on the music. So I was an only duckling altogether. I was the only one to carry on the Gunn tradition.

---

1. Pat, with his brothers Tommy and John, formed Mamas Boys, a rock band which lasted from 1980 to 1992. They played as Celtus from 1992 to 2001 and began to move more towards traditional music. Their most recent album as Celtus was "Moon Child" with Sony Records, UK. They toured internationally with both bands. All this time, Pat continued to play fiddle, and John, the uilleann pipes.

Hugh Gunn, Molly Gunn (wife), Katie Gunn (John's mother) and Uncle Frank Gunn, a noted singer.

Left to right: Master Flynn, Uncle Hugh Gunn, Cormac Lunny and John McManus.

And did she play as well?

John: She did, a little bit, but she was a marvellous lilter. And Uncle Hugh Gunn, that I learnt the fiddle off, I'd go down to him and I'd learn the tune and play it to her and she could lilt the tune exactly as he played it. Before she went to America, he [Hugh] was a fiddler that went from house to house playing at sprees long ago, and she went along with him and she lilted along, and he played the fiddle and she knew all his tunes, you see.

That was her brother?

John: That was her brother, that's right. Then, as I say, we came home from America in 1932 – I was born in '25 – we came home in '32 then to the old homestead here. My father died then in 1939, and that left myself and my mother alone here. And it left us in a bit of a predicament: I didn't know how to do anything. Well I'd look after the cows we had here – we had six cows at the time – and my mother'd be down in the bog and I'd be down in the field trying to help with the spuds. I took up the music anyway. I suppose I was about eight years old when I started the fiddle, and I got a mandolin then from a cousin of mine that had come from England. So I was becoming a kind of famous around the country, me and Uncle Hugh playing, the two of us playing the two fiddles together, and then drop the fiddle and play the mandolin – the mandolin was an unheard of thing then. So I was about seventeen and my name was rightly known, well you know, just in the country houses, the country places, and they decided they'd start a band in Derrylin, a dance band. So they came for me. I was about seventeen at the time and I was mad to get joining. I went up and I brought my mandolin. The first money I got was two shillings – I was made up. That was the start of the band then. That was in 1942.

I think it was in 1946 then, we were playing in Derrylin AOH [Ancient Order of Hibernians] Hall. Then we got down to Kinawley, and then we were getting to Teemore, which was branching out. Well, John Joe McManus that lived up the road, a cousin of mine, he was the boss of the band – I was the boss of the band when we were on stage and he was the man that took the bookings. So he says, 'Do you know, John, most of the bands has an instrument called a saxophone. I think we should try and get one.' And I says, 'Who'd play it?' And he says, 'Sure you can, or you can try it anyway.' So we gathered money together, playing here and there and when we got some together, we headed for Cavan. There was a music shop there and Farrell was the name of the people that owned the music shop. We went into this shop anyway and just asked for a saxophone. Well, he had none of them, as I called them, a "crooked saxophone". He had only one saxophone, a straight one – a soprano sax as I found out later – it was like a clarinet. I had seen a great band from Clones called the Pat MacMahon Dance Band and they had a sax I thought was beautiful. Anyway, I began to play bits on the one from Cavan. I don't know how my mother's head stuck it at all, because there were some droll sounds coming out of it. But after a couple of months, I had four or five tunes on it and I was playing a few of them in the band. We decided then that it wasn't good enough. I was still harping on about the crooked saxophone. We set off again, and Belfast this time, Matchetts in Belfast. So we went down there and there was any amount of these crooked saxophones and we bought an alto. Brought it home anyway. It cost seventy-eight pounds – big money then. We were a long time getting it together playing nights here and there and I started to play, but I found out – I didn't find out until I went to a dance one night in Derrylin to see Pat MacMahon playing – I was playing with the mouthpiece upside down. I knew so little about it. I had it up instead of down, but I was knocking toppin' music out of it, or I thought I was. So then they decided they'd get a piano accordion. So one of the other lads, Pat O'Hara, a buddy of mine, he's still alive in America, he took it, but Pat could only play on the white keys, he couldn't get in on sharps or flats. It was a disaster. But he couldn't change onto my key that I was playing on the saxophone, and I couldn't change onto his and we were in a mess. So somebody suggested that there was such a thing as a C Melody, and if we got that, it'd go along with the accordion. So we bought this kind of a C Melody – ah now, the sound was horrible – but it played along with the

John McManus from the Starlight Dance Band days.

accordion and I could play on his key and he could play on mine. So I didn't like it at all, but I said to myself, now John you'll have to really learn how to play the saxophone and change keys. So we had an auld wireless in the window at the time and I used to switch it on every morning. And there was the big bands from London – Joe Loss, Lou Praeger, Stanley Black, Harry Gold and his Pieces of Eight – and here I was with my saxophone up to the radio, and I'd try and imitate them, and when they'd change keys, I'd try and change keys. So that's how I learnt. So I got that I could change along with the piano accordion. He didn't have to change at all, I done the changing.

And we done great. We did a lot of nights around Sligo. Sligo was a great county for us altogether. I remember one night we were late going to a hall in Sligo. Jimmy Gunn was our taxi driver, and we got a puncture or something, and they started to boo us when we went in. The priest, he was ranting and raving. So Terry Carron took him to one side. 'To tell you the truth,' he says, 'what happened is that when we were coming over, didn't the B Men stop us and they held us up and they were nearly taking us to the barracks and taking all our instruments.' Well, the priest announced this off the stage and sure we were heroes. We could do no wrong at all.

[*Tea arriving*] *You were saying one time you played* The Soldiers' Song *in an Orange Hall?*

John: Well they had this dance in the Orange Hall. They were stuck for music, their band had let them down so they called for us – sent us word would we come up and fill in for the band.

So we went up and played anyway, and at the end of the night I jumped up and we banged into *The Soldier's Song* and John Joe Mac was prodding me with the drumstick in the back. 'What the hell's wrong with you?' says I. Well, the people, they understood of course, they just laughed.

Valerie: And you heard about the rosary, I suppose, and the tango?

Where was that?

Valerie: That was over in Scotstown and we were playing one-steps and old-time waltzes and *The Siege Of Ennis* and stuff like that, but then we thought we'd throw in a tango. We were advancing in our music, you see [*laughs at this*], playing sambas and all that, and all of a sudden, the priest shouts, 'Stop! Stop! You're not playing any of that kind of stuff here. No sambas or tangos or anything like that, or occasions of sin. Do you know what we'll do now?' he says. 'We'll all say the rosary.' In the middle of the whole dance! Us crowd up on the stage, we had to join in. And no difference in the steps anyway – they didn't know how to do a samba.

And what was the one-step?

John: It was march time... two steps forward and one back.

And what would you play for that?

John: Well you would... [*John lilts*]

Valerie: And then they dance with the bicycle clips in.

John: God aye, they mightn't take the bicycle clips out at all. And then, if you wanted to impress a girl, you left the bicycle clips in your top pocket so she knew she had a lift home on the bar of the bike. And 1952 then – this appeared [*laughs as he refers to Valerie joining the band*]. Owen Murphy, a cousin of mine too, he was the singer, but his sister was getting married and he had to go to the wedding, so we were stuck for a singer. So John Joe McManus came down. 'I'll get you a lassie down the road that's a great singer.' So we went down and talked to the mother and they weren't enamoured. They didn't want to let her out at all, but anyway, we talked them round in the end.

Valerie: I was auditioned up in Derrylin Hall. John was kind of woman-shy at the time. I was sitting down in the hall after doing the audition and when he got down off the stage to sit down beside me to chat me, the rest of them were all standing with their mouths open. They couldn't believe it because he was a bit shy that way. But he kept the chat going after that because we ended up getting married.

You married the leading lady, John?

John: That's right. That was in '52.

And was your family musical too, Valerie?

John McManus on fiddle with Barney Fitzgerald.

Valerie: Yes, my Uncle Matt was a classical violinist and my aunt was the most beautiful singer. She got an offer to sing [in accompaniment to] silent movies, but the family put the foot down... they were really against this. This was in County Meath. She was a singer in a choir and the choir took her up to Dublin to do this rehearsal. Somebody heard about it and she got an offer (she often showed it to us), but the parents wouldn't let her. They thought that was only for low-class people.

So you were married in '52?

John: '52. That's right.

You were ten years going at that stage.

John: That's right. That was in '52. Aye, until '62. I was from '42 until '62 in the band. So then we went into the Carnegie Showband and this was a band made up from The Red

Harp of Erin Céilidhe Band. Left to right: Pat McManus, Cormac Lunny, John McManus, Tommy McManus, Jason Gunn, Tommy Maguire, Paddy Gunn, Peggy Burke. Back, left to right: John Patrick Brennan, Francis Kellagher.

Sunbeam from Swad and The Starlight. It was a great band. I was playing tenor sax; Andy Maguire from Irvinestown was on trombone and Glen [*a cousin of Ciaran*] Curran on trumpet. We had Jazzie McGovern on the drums. It didn't go very far. But as showbands were at the time, it would have held its own with any of them. We practised for seven weeks at Lent and we were ready to go on the road at the end of it. We went to the Silver Sandal every single night of the week for seven weeks and we went out with a bang. It was fantastic. We played before Larry Cunningham and the Mighty Avons, and Larry had this beautiful tenor sax and they were swaying, playing and walking around the stage and prancing around and I says to Larry, 'That's a beautiful saxophone.' 'It's all right, John,' he says, 'if I could play it.'

You were saying that Tommy Gunn was with you at the start.

John: Tommy Gunn was with the céilidhe band. That was the Harp of Erin Céilidhe Band. That's his photograph above there.

Was that the same time as The Starlight? You had the two going at the same time?

John: That's right.

And the people here in The Harp of Erin? [Valerie lists the names of the members of The Harp of Erin – see opposite. Tommy Vetty Maguire also played with this band. One of his tunes, Tommy Vetty's Waltz *later became widely known through an Altan recording.]*

[We looked at the photograph of The Starlight Dance Band next. John pointed out the music stands and said that they were only there for show as none of them read music. The band organiser felt that it looked better but had to remind them occasionally to make some use of them.]

John: John Joe would come to the side of the stage an odd time and he'd say, 'Boys, turn the page now and again.' They'd be upside down, more than likely.

And what kind of songs were you singing?

John: Oh, the ones that were popular at the time. Sure, the only way... I hadn't even a radio at this time, and the only way I could get them... I had a cousin in the women's military during the war and she was down in Bangor, and they had the army radios there, you see. So Roseanne, a cousin, Roseanne Murphy, she was in the ATS – that was the women's military at the time – she used to get the whole tunes off them and she'd phone the shop up here and the shopkeeper'd send down word for me to go up quick, my cousin was on,

Starlight Dance Band. Left to right: John Gunn, John McManus, Brian Gallagher, Sean Gallagher, Francie Ingram, Owen Murphy.

and she'd lilt the tune or sing the song across the phone to me and I'd learn it and I'd get the shop girl to write down the words.

So Roseanne would learn it too?

John: Sure – this is the only way I had of getting them.

And then you worked out an arrangement?

John: I'd work out some arrangement then.

You must have had a great ear.

John: I had a great ear at that time.

And you could just pick up things off the radio?

John: Just on one shot at that time.

Valerie: The strange thing was that he couldn't listen to it and then sit down and play it. Two days later – it just clicked in after that time. He would leave it alone until it would start to come together in his head.

John: One night down in McConnell's – Cathal's that is – there was strange fiddlers there and musicians there from all over. 'Boys, I want to tell you something,' he [Cathal] says. 'If there's a tune you don't want to part with, don't play it in front of John, because it'll be gone.'

And, when you heard the tune on the radio, would you think about it in those couple of days?

John: No, I'd forget about it, and just the thing would come back to me.

Valerie: Sometimes we'd be coming home long ago on the bicycles from Mass. I'd think he had fallen out with me or something because he wouldn't be talking and I'd be going on, 'Oh don't talk, don't talk 'til I get in.' In and down would come the fiddle. Then, once he played it, then he was sure. But the whole thing was going on in his head, and if I spoke to him it'd put it out of his head.

John: I couldn't play by notes, not if I was to die, and I tried it twice or three times. There was a wee classical violinist who was teaching in Enniskillen and I thought I'd go in and try and learn something about the notes. And of course, I could play the fiddle well at the time, traditional stuff, and he told me different notes on different lines, and I'd agree with him. I didn't want to show him that I didn't understand and he says, 'Now you know enough I'll put down this bit of a tune for you. You can have it for me the next time you come back.' 'All right,' says I. 'But do you know what you'll do? You play it over.' So he played it over and I lifted the fiddle and played it for him. 'Go home,' he says. 'Don't bother coming back.'

Valerie: Cathal McConnell was told the same, to go home, that he couldn't be taught.

John: I remember being in a flute band...

You were playing flute?

John: Aye, of course. It was a flute band in Derrylin and we were all training up in the AOH Hall in Derrylin, and they were all up at the blackboard reading off the notes and of course I got Arthur James to play them for me. Now, this night they weren't getting on well together, the tune just wasn't coming together right and they were making a real muck of the harmony. He says, 'Why can't yous play it like John? He just goes up there and reads it off the board. Can't yous do the same?' I played the clarinet then, which was different again from the saxophone. So I sort of mastered it in a kind of way; I used to play it in the band.

You met Josie, didn't you, Josie McDermott?

John: O God! I did, aye. That was in Connor's Cross in Sligo.

He must have had a very similar background to yourself, saxophone and traditional and so on.

John: That's right... these people used to come to the dances with The Starlight, and they found out that I was a traditional man too. But after the dance would be all over – the dances all ended at twelve o'clock that time – four or five of them would get together. I'd have the fiddle as well and we'd have a bit of a session until three or four o'clock in the morning. That's where I met Josie. I didn't know at that time that he was blind.

Valerie: Or for years after.

John: That's right, for years after. He was a flute player... a lovely player and a lovely style and a great singer... and a gentleman as well.

Valerie: Who was the piper we went up to see in Sligo, what was his name?

John: He was Dolan. He was a brother of Packie Dolan and a lovely piper. At the time, John [*their son*] was learning the uilleann pipes. We took him up and he showed John a few things. The pipes John got were from Tommy Rourke – he's from Lisnaskea but he lives in Corby now. He was a great piper, him, and the other man from Roslea, Sean McAloon. And then there was another fella, Martin from Lisnaskea, although I never saw him or heard him.

Valerie: Who was the piper, the one with the long fingers who said that he heard that the fairies were teaching in Fermanagh when he heard Tommy Rourke?

John: That was Johnny Doran and he was coming through Lisnaskea this day, and he heard of Tommy Rourke playing, so he made it his business to go to Tommy Rourke's and he says when he's leaving, 'The fairies have been in touch with that man.' That's what he told other people when he left... he didn't tell Tommy that, now.

Were the house dances very popular?

Valerie: Well, on Ash Wednesday they took out partying from one house to another... and there was a man left one party and was heading home in the morning not feeling great, and there was a sow and she was lying up with her belly to the sun. 'God!' says he. 'What would I give to be a sow!'

John: And I remember one time there was a hooley up in Owen Murphy's, and me and my mother came down the road that morning about eight o'clock and we milked the cows, and she fed the hens and done a few things around the house, and back we went to the party and it continued.

Valerie: And Uncle Hugh's wedding, how long did it last?

John: Uncle Hugh's wedding went on for seven weeks.

And where was the poitín made?

John: Oh, down the bog there, a few fields away.

And would it have been all poitín then?

John: Well, sometimes there was a barrel got in the pub. The expert would be called in then to tap the barrel, because there was a knack in tapping it right.

Valerie: I often heard Granny saying they used to go out and stand on the step at night with their coats on and say, 'Which house will we go to?' because there was a party in nearly every house. They had to choose which house to go to.

Plenty of social life?

Valerie: No shortage of social life at all.

John: There'd be the odd row too. I was playing at a mummers' dance one night...

Valerie: These were the Fenians and the "Hibs" [Hibernians].

John: And they were called "Tets" long ago, that was the Fenians.

Valerie: And the Hibernians were the "Mollys" – the Molly Maguires.

John: And they didn't agree at all, good nor bad... they were far worse enemies than the Catholics or Protestants, they hated each other. Anyway, we went out and we mummed around the country before Christmas and got a bit of money together, eighteen or twenty pounds, which was a lot of money.

Valerie: And then there was always a party.

John: There'd be a party then... and it was in a man's house, J—— C——'s down the road. So the party was in full swing, I was playing, and they were out dancing. J—— C—— came over to me – he was a Fenian, you see, a Tet. He says, 'Play us The White Cockade'... No, he says. 'Play us The Green Cockade.' And of course, my whole descendants were all Hibernians. They were the White Cockades, you see, so it was like waving a rag to a bull.

Valerie: Not to you.

John: Not to me. I didn't give a damn, but J—— M—— was there and he seen J—— C—— and he suspected what J—— C—— was at and he came over to me. 'What,' he says, 'was C—— saying to you?' 'Ah,' says I, 'nothing much,' and I kept playing away. 'Come on,' he says, 'he was saying something.' 'Ah,' says I, 'he wanted me to play The Green Cockade.' 'He what!' says he... He made for him. Out went C——, down through the hall door, into the room, J—— M—— after him and there was a big tablecloth on the table; utensils, food, everything... C—— got a hold of the tablecloth and whipped all off, and they fought out of the room, into the hallway and out the door and the rest of the Fenians were there joining in to help J—— C——, and the Hibernians helped J—— M——. There was murder, and then they lay in wait. When the dance was over, about six o'clock in the morning, we set off for home... but J—— M—— and the Hibernians lay in wait for the Fenians coming up the road 'til they could wallop them there and then.[2]

And what kind of dances would you have done that time?

John: *The Eight-Hand Reel* and the *Square Reel*, that'd be four, and the *Four-Hand Reel* and then there was *The Wexford Reel*.

Valerie: And I think it was only danced in Fermanagh, funnily enough, although it was called *The Wexford Reel*.

John: I talked to a lot of people and they never heard tell of it... just four people dancing, two men and two women and then the sets, the ordinary sets.

Valerie: That was eight.

John: And then hornpipes and flings and barn dances, and the odd old-time waltz thrown in... you could be playing from eight o'clock at night until eight o'clock in the morning so there'd be two waltzes thrown in... that'd be just the country house dance. And then of course the songs, there could be songs that'd go on for fifteen or twenty minutes.

And recitations?

John: No, very few recitations.

[*The discussion moved on to local songs. John suddenly remembered one about his grandfather, Red Pat Gunn.*]

---

2. This factionalism, or infighting, seems to have persisted longer in Fermanagh than in most other places. In Robin Morton's *Come Day, Go Day, God Send Sunday*, John Maguire from Roslea, who wrote a song about the Molly Maguires, says:

> Sometimes the songs didn't suit several organisations, do you see, in the country. It could raise trouble in a house or a hall if you did sing a song. It could raise a wee disturbance even among our own population, Catholic population. They didn't agree at that time at all, there would be plenty of battles between them. I seen it myself. I seen me singing a song away down at Cooneen, it ris trouble.

According to Robin Morton: 'The Mollys tended to join the Ancient Order of Hibernians... [which] backed the treaty setting up the Irish Free State in 1921.' The more separatist tradition was presumably represented by the Fenians or Tets in the incident John McManus describes. How much this factionalism was about politics, or about old family feuds, or a confused mixture of both, is unclear now.

Henry Glassie in *Passing the Time* (based on Bellanaleck) was told similar stories:

> The party of compromise, the Molly Maguires, was considered traitorous by the "rebels" of Sinn Féin. That was no abstract sentiment. When the band on the road beat *The Green Cockade*, or men in the pub sang Charlie Farmer's song, *You'll Find Lots Of The Blackguard In Molly Maguires*, they were consolidating against their neighbours.

John's grandfather, Red Pat Gunn of the ferry boat.

John: And then there was another song that was made of my grandfather, Pat Gunn. He ran a ferry boat from the lough meadows here to Lisnaskea.

Was that the man you called Red Pat Gunn?

John: Red Pat Gunn... so there was a song made about the boat. It used to carry eighteen people... it was a rowboat. [John and Valerie sing]:

Pat Gunn's Boat

Valerie & John McManus

1. There's a boat just now launched at Knockninny, whose equal has never been seen;
   And nobody's christened her yet, but I call her the Long Ferry Queen.
   Indeed she's a beautiful picture, all youse that are up for the fun,
   Just take a short trip to Knockninny, and sail down to 'Skea with Pat Gunn.
   CHORUS:
   So boys aye and girls so hearty, all youse that are up for the fun,
   Just take a short trip to Knockninny, and sail down to 'Skea with Pat Gunn.

2. Indeed she's a beautiful picture, to see her float on the Lough like a swan,
   And then there's her fine steward rowers, whose like is not under the sun.
   The captain he stands at the stern, with his hand on the tiller so true,
   And fo'ward you'll see old Tom Corrigan, who was lost in the Old Bug-A-Boo. [3]
   CHORUS

3. An old maid who lived down in the valley, whose name I'm not going to tell,
   She swore that she never would marry, for men they were only a sell;
   When she saw our fine boat put in motion, she thought she would ne'er cease to run,
   Till she landed below at Knockninny, to sail down to 'Skea with Pat Gunn.
   CHORUS

4. To see her return in the evening, as our beautiful boat sails along,
   The boys and the girls all together, would liven the way with a song;
   Mavroon when she comes to the landing, the boys to the Hotel would run,
   To give us a 'céad míle fáilte', and a rousing good cheer for Pat Gunn.
   CHORUS

---

3. From *The Bug-A-Boo* in *The Second Book of Irish Ballads* by James N Healy, Mercier 1962. The author comments it may have been "a canal ballad". John and Valerie's song, composed by a local family, may have been a parody of the above but it is very different in every other way and has its own air.

Old friends, Cathal McConnell (left) and John McManus with *The Gunn Book*.

Sharon Creasey, who transcribed the tunes and songs for this publication, examines *The Gunn Book*.

CHAPTER 2
The Gunn Book

This is a manuscript of dance tunes written down by John Gunn in the middle years of the 19th century. It is handwritten with the dipped ink pen of the time, and the cursive style of handwriting in the tune titles shows all the signs of a trained and well-practised hand. The tunes themselves are beautifully transcribed and still perfectly readable. The collection is hand-bound. The manuscript pages are in single leaves, stamped "London Improved", and the whole is stitched together. Both John McManus and John Reihill point out that the various Gunn families had many trades, including tailoring, and the stitching together of this volume is expertly done. The front and back covers are made up of light brown paper covered with black cloth. Through use, the cloth has worn through, torn in places, and has been patched with a similar material. The book has a strap made of what was probably originally a plain light material (like that used for lining a garment) that has darkened over time. One possible explanation for the strap is that it was used for carrying the book around. Perhaps John Gunn, who was a fiddle player, carried the manuscript with him when playing here and there, although it seems unlikely that he would treat it in such a casual fashion. Another possibility is that the strap was simply used for hanging the book on a wall when not in use.

The forty-three-page collection contains 178 tunes: 105 reels, twenty-eight hornpipes, forty-one jigs and four miscellaneous pieces. It is evidently the work of one person, as the style of transcription and the handwriting are consistent up to the final four miscellaneous tunes. It would appear that someone

John Reihill's boat heading out towards Iniscorkish Island on Upper Lough Erne.

attempted to add to the collection at some point and included *Believe Me If All These Enduring Young Charms* and *Love's Young Dream* from *Moore's Irish Melodies*. Apart from this, the collection is entirely the work of John Gunn. It is organised according to tune type; starting with hornpipes, then jigs, and followed by reels. More jigs appear in the second half, and at the very end, but reels predominate.

The manuscript is not regarded as the property of any single individual but as part of a wider family legacy. Some years ago it was passed into the hands of John Reihill whose aunt was married to a grandson of John Gunn's. John Reihill and his wife live on Inishcorkish Island on Upper Lough Erne, not far from Derrylin. They are the only people who continue to live, and to make a living, on one of Lough Erne's islands. They farm and, during the summer months, run a restaurant for passing cruisers. John describes himself as the "custodian of the book".

John Gunn was a direct ancestor of John McManus of Knockninny. He lived in the townland of Corratistune (about two miles from Knockninny) and is believed to have been a farmer. His house, close to the lakeshore, looks out over the waters of Upper Lough Erne to Trasna Island. It was there, in run-down condition, until very recent years.

The Griffith Valuation[4] of 1862, for the townland of Corratistune, included a John Gunn, Sr. who leased, from the Earl of Enniskillen, twelve acres, three roods and eighty-one perches, with "house and offices", all to the rateable value of £8 – 10s – 0d. In terms of land held, he was one of the better-off in the townland. The corresponding map in the Griffith Valuation, Sheet 39 (Val 2A/4/39A) of the Ordnance Survey Map of County Fermanagh, shows this holding to be where the remains of his home, shown to me by John McManus, can still be seen. John McManus and John Reihill provided the following genealogy. They have a much more complete family tree in their memories, but only those who feature in some way in this publication are included here.

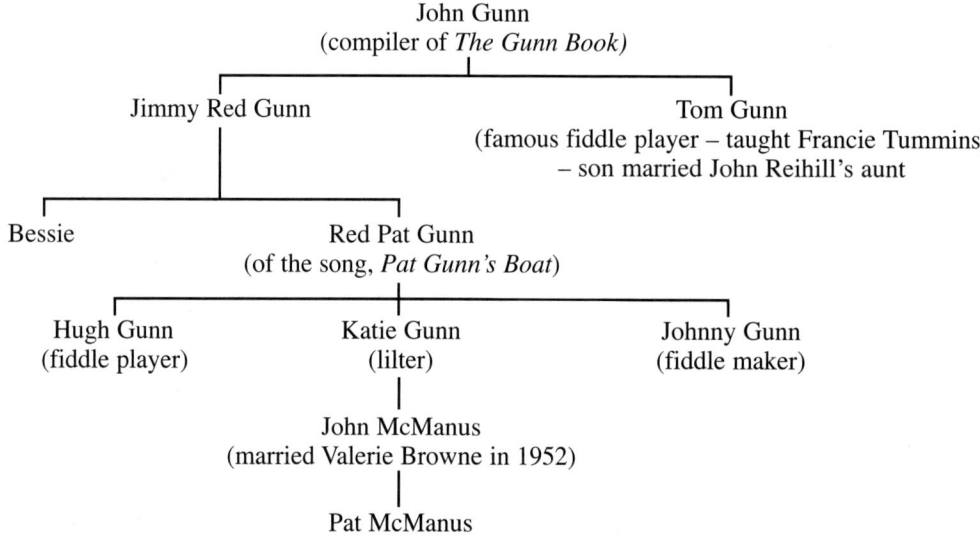

---

4. My thanks to Margaret Kane of Enniskillen Library who provided this information and much more on local publications over the years.

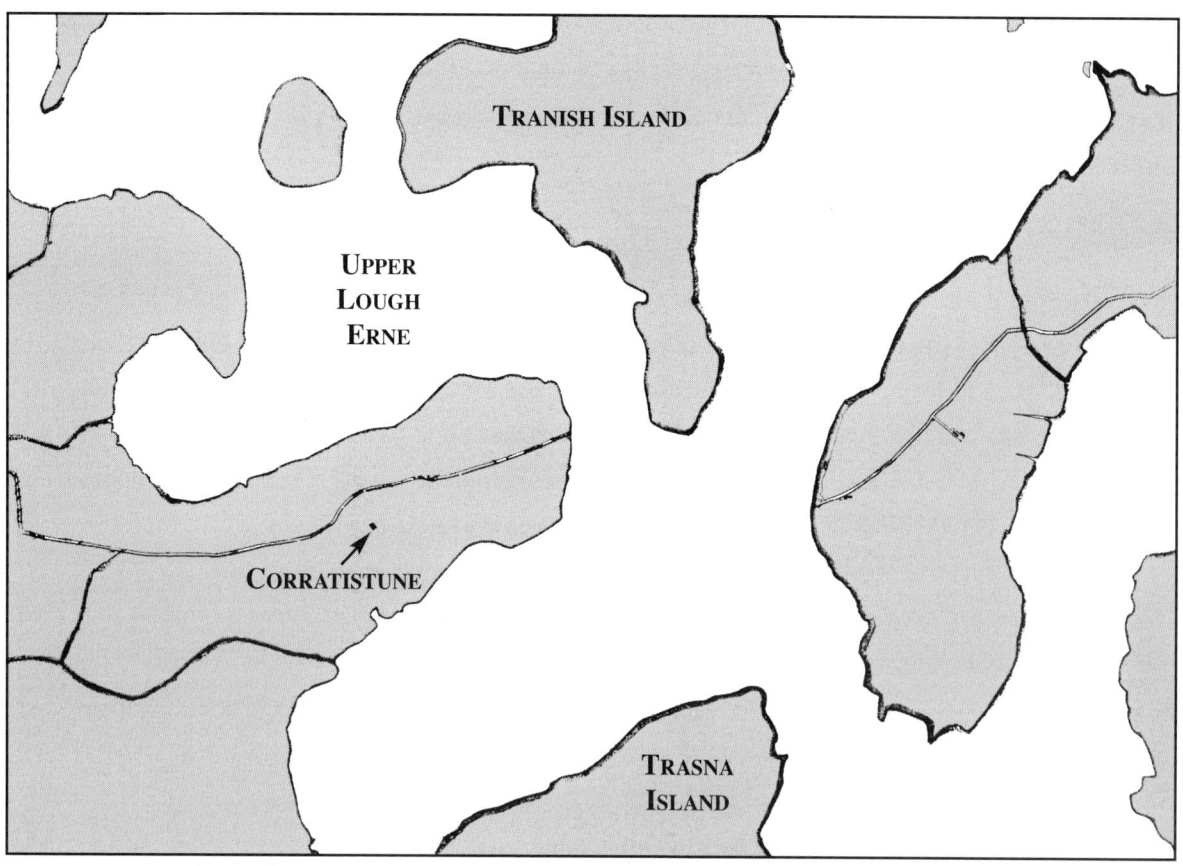
Where John Gunn's farm house stood until recently. Trasna Island in background.
Map taken from Griffith Valuation 1862.

Fintan McManus, cousin of Pat McManus. Like John McManus, Fintan's mother was also Gunn.

We know from John McManus that Old John Gunn (sometimes referred to as the Original John Gunn in order to distinguish him from other John Gunns in the area) was a fiddle player. His fiddle, in a poor state of repair, once came into his (John McManus') possession and he took it to his Uncle Johnny, the fiddle maker, to have it repaired.

> John McManus: I did, but it's gone for good now anyway. I went up – Pat was doing a project for his school on *The Gunn Book* – I went up to the house in Corratistune. This old woman, Mrs Gunn, was there and I asked her (she had the book) could I get the loan. She says, 'And welcome, John, and there's something else here now, and I know you're a direct descendant, you're the one plays the fiddle, you're the one to have it – this is John Gunn's fiddle.' Now, it was just in ribbons, in bits, but I was delighted to have it and brought it home anyway. Ahhhh, it lay in the attic for years, and then I was telling Johnny Gunn, that was Johnny Gunn that made the fiddles, another descendant up beside Corratistune, so, 'God, John,' he says, 'you should bring it up and we'll put it together even if it was never played.' So, I brought it up to him in an old fiddle box – it was just in bits – but Johnny died.

The fiddle disappeared with the changes that followed. John later returned the manuscript to Mrs Gunn. She was an aunt of John Reihill's, and before she died she gave the manuscript to him for safekeeping. That is how *The Gunn Book* came to Iniscorkish Island.

John McManus had two other interesting pieces of information about John Gunn. He said that he was reported to be something of a dandy. His Uncle Hugh often described him as such.

> John McManus: Oh yes... it was my Uncle Hugh told me this now and people told him... a stovepipe hat and a green coat with tails, and a coloured waistcoat and the britches and stockings. That was his dress.

Also, according to John's Uncle Hugh, he learned his tunes from a travelling fiddle player.

> John McManus: That's right. There used to come a travelling fiddle player around the country, playing in your house and my house, playing for the dances, although we never got his name, he was just called Celter. So John Gunn would go whenever Celter came round the country and he'd go to hear him and jot down the tunes. Where he came from, nobody ever could tell. Donegal possibly. There's an awful Donegal tendency in them tunes, and when you listen to Johnny Doherty and them playing, it's even the same bowing, very flamboyant bowing, you know, from toe to tip. You see the fellas up in Clare now, and it's only the tip, they do it all with the fingers... but the Northern style, it's with the bow. The triplets are done with the bow.

It seems likely that "Celter" is a form, or a local pronunciation, of the Irish word "ceoltóir", or musician. Travelling musicians were certainly a feature of the time (and possibly more of the century before) and they are described in many accounts with details of their circuit and what they earned. In an earlier period, before John Gunn's time, they would have come to accompany a dancing master,[5] but John McManus never heard anyone mention this.

The bowing style described by John McManus is his own style and that of his son, Pat. Cathal McConnell says that Tommy Gunn used the same method of playing triplets, described by John, when playing *Lady Anne Montgomery* and that he (Tommy) learned this from Francie Tummins of Tranish Island. Francie, in turn, as already mentioned, was taught by Tom Gunn (a son of Old John Gunn).

Fortunately, one page in *The Gunn Book* is dated "St Patrick's Day 1865". It is likely that John Gunn was elderly by this time. We know that his grandson, Red Pat Gunn of the song, was married to a Mary Ann McManus in 1863. He was clearly collecting music for quite some time, possibly for much of his life, and he may very well have already started by the time the third volume of Edward Bunting's collections appeared in 1840.

A brief glance at some of the dates, and the nature of the early collections of Irish music, will help to give an idea of the significance of John Gunn's collection. Before the latter part of the 19th century, the collecting of Irish music was sporadic and the best-known collections did not focus on the dance music of the time. Edward Bunting's work was by far the best known with his first volume, *Ancient Irish Music,* appearing in 1796 but, as we know, he was attempting to collect and preserve the older harp music and the associated songs. *Petrie's Ancient Music of Ireland*, published in 1855, consisted mostly of airs and songs which were part of the harping tradition.

You get the feeling sometimes that the old school of harpers, and those who collected from them, had no great regard for dance tunes. Arthur O'Neill, a blind harper from Tyrone who became Bunting's main source, tells the story of another Tyrone harper, Ned McAleer, who referred to dance tunes as "servants' music" and had to be defended from the wrath of the servants present.[6] Dance tunes were being published of course, often as part of a collection of songs or other music. Neales' *A Collection of the Most Celebrated Irish Tunes*, possibly the first to concentrate on dance tunes, was published in Dublin in 1736. The first Lee collection of tunes by the piping rector from Limerick, Rev Jackson, was published in 1774. Brysson published *A Curious Collection of Favourite Tunes* with fifty Irish airs in 1790 in Edinburgh. Cooke's *Twenty-One Favourite Irish Airs* appeared in Dublin in 1793. In 1800,

---

5. Breathnach provides this description of one dancing master: 'Caroline hat, swallow-tail coat and tight knee-breeches, white stockings and turn-pumps, cane with a silver head and silk tassel – thus accoutred, the dancing master was obviously a cut above the wandering piper or fiddler. He was a person to be treated with due deference by his pupils.' Breandan Breathnach, *Folk Music and Dances of Ireland*, p. 49.

6. At one time, when poor Ned McAleer went to a Counsellor Stewart of Baillieborough, in the County Cavan, which time Harry Fitzsimmons, the harper, was there. He was ordered to play in the hall as a specimen, where there were some tailors then at work for the servants. [He] began to play some Irish tunes, jigs, reels, etc. Mrs Stewart, after some time, came from the parlour to the hall, and told him she was much disappointed, as some of her own countrymen could excel him. McAleer, chagrined, started up and exclaimed, 'Madam, as you were pleased to order me to play in the hall, I played you tailors' and servants' music, which would otherwise be different.' 'Damn your soul, you trumping rascal,' says one of the snips, bouncing off the floor, and was going to destroy poor McAleer with his goose, and if it was not for some interference, he was determined to avenge the mighty insult. *Annals of the Irish Harpers*, p. 154. (Includes the Memoirs of Arthur O'Neill.)

O'Farrell's *Pocket Companion*, a large collection of Irish music for union pipes, was published in London. There were other private collections. In the Irish Traditional Music Archive there is a handwritten collection of dance tunes by Rev J Quinn dated 1844. One of his jigs, *The Rights Of Irishmen*,[7] appears in *The Gunn Book* as *The Rights Of Irish*. However, the scale of publication in the first half of the 19th century does not appear to have been anything like that of Scotland, where publications such as *A Selection of Scottish, English, Irish and Foreign Airs Adapted to the Fife, Violin, or German Flute*, by James Aird, (Glasgow: 1782–1801 in six vols.) appeared in great numbers. Tomás Ó Canainn draws attention to Mulholland's *Collection of Ancient Irish Airs* published in Belfast in the first decade of the 19th century. It contains about eighty airs. Collections proliferated later in the century, culminating, by the turn of the century, in O'Neill's *The Music of Ireland* (1,850 tunes) in 1903 and his more widely used *Dance Music of Ireland* (1,001 Gems) in 1907.

Nevertheless, at the time when John Gunn was noting down his tunes (and we can only conjecture that he had been doing it for a quite some years before 1865), there is little evidence of dance tunes being collected in any systematic fashion in the northern half of the country. His collection, for this reason alone, is of particular interest, and a closer look at some of the tunes reveals its distinctive character.

The manuscript, as might be expected, contains many tunes which are familiar from the general repertoire, along with many that are less familiar. What is surprising, is the number of little-known tunes. *The Harvest Home* is there and *The Liverpool Hornpipe*. Two of those which feature on the CD (played by Annette Owens with Brian McGrath), *Leyeer's Hornpipe* and *Miss Adams' Hornpipe*, are not known generally, although the latter is listed in *The Scottish Fiddle Music Index* as being in the collection of a William Campbell, who published between 1790 and 1817. *The Rights Of Irish*, a jig, is

Annette Owens.

---

7. Quinn MS, p. 10 – this is a manuscript found in a house in Abbeyshaule, County Longford, some pages dated 1845 and 1846. It has never been published. It is now with the Irish Traditional Music Archive, Merrion Square, Dublin.

to be found in The Quinn Manuscript, dated 1844, but is not a known tune. *Wellington's Advance* appears in O'Neill's *The Dance Music of Ireland* (1907). *The Boys Of Portaferry* is listed in *The Breandan Breathnach Index* as *The Sporting Boy* and *The Tin Whistle Reel*. *Rory O'Moore* is widely known and appears under many titles. *I Lost My Love And I Care Not* is an interesting entry in that Mick Hoy's humorous song, *Charlie McNeil*, is set to the same air. It is almost certainly of Scottish origin and is listed in the *Scottish Fiddle Music Index* as *I Lost My Love*. *Squeeze Your Thighs* we know as *The Munster Buttermilk*, although *The Gunn Book* version has five parts rather than the usual three. *Johnny Going To France* is in the *Breathnach Index* as *Jenny Picking Cockles*. *Over The Water To Charley* appears as *Seán Buí, Yellow John, Orange John* or *Thady Brady*. A very small number, including *Lady Gardener's Troop Reel* and *The Grand Spy* are listed as strathspeys in *The Scottish Index*. In the same index, *The Downshire Reel* appears as a quickstep and *The Copenhagen Reel* as a waltz. The title *Sally Kelly's Reel* appears in *The Northern Fiddler*, but the tune is different.

There are eleven Jackson tunes: nine jigs and two reels. *Jackson's Morning Brush* is familiar to us, but others, such as *Jackson's Postchaise* and *Jackson's Walk To Limerick*, are not. As already mentioned, Jackson's tunes were published in *The Lee Collection* in 1790, but there were two Jacksons, both pipers, and accounts of them differ. The Limerick piper, Walker Jackson, lived in the parish of Ballingarry in a residence known as "The Turret". Bunting recorded Jackson as being from Monaghan, and O'Neill quotes a correspondent to the effect that Piper Jackson lived at Creeve, near Ballybay in County Monaghan. Breathnach, in an article in *A Journal of Irish Music*, gives a bewildering (and very learned) account of Walker Jackson's tunes and other titles associated with them. Two of the eleven from *The Gunn Book* are listed in other collections, and Breathnach attributes five of the eleven to Walker Jackson. Presumably, he attributes the others to the northern Jackson, although he states, very forcefully that, 'It is most unlikely that Jackson (either one) composed a tenth of the tunes attributed to him.' Whether this is the case or not, Jackson's tunes were clearly popular early in the 19th century in this part of Fermanagh, as they form a significant part of John Gunn's collection. It is reasonable to assume that most of these, and particularly the more obscure ones, such as *Jackson's Dream* and *Jackson's Mistake*, came from the northern Jackson and were played around the Derrylin area.

Reels dominate this collection and many are obscure. *The Milltown Lasses*, a particularly attractive tune (played by Brenda McCann on CD, vol. 1), is one of these. *The Ereshire Lasses* and *Lady Lubeck* are unfamiliar, although the latter has similarities to the tune of *Follow Me Down To Carlow*. *The Humours of Swanlinbar* (in Cavan, but on the Fermanagh border close to Derrylin) is a very unusual tune and, like many of the others, previously unknown to any of us. The first part of *Sir Edward Gunn's Reel* is very similar to *Matt Molloy's Reel*, but with a completely different second part and played in the key of C. *The Poor Scholar* is most likely an earlier version of the well-known *The Scholar*. *The Grand Spy* we know as *The Graf Spee*, and *Ryan's Rant*, which is similar to the first and third parts of *Granny's Gravel Walks*, was part of Mick Hoy's repertoire.

We know from the playing of John McManus that these tunes were once well known in the area. John never learned to read music (he never needed to – see p. 15) so he never made use of the manuscript. He

Brenda McCann.

learned from his Uncle Hugh, who did read music, and John, with his son Pat, regularly plays tunes such as *The Primrose Lass, The Priest In His Boots, The Collegians Of Glasgow* and others, exactly as found in *The Gunn Book*. Tommy Gunn, as we have seen, played tunes which are to be found in the manuscript, as did Pee Flanagan[8] and as do John Joe Maguire and Cathal McConnell – although not to anything like the same extent as John McManus. What is important about this is that it indicates a collector who was noting down what he heard being played around him and he was clearly drawing on a rich source.

This collection gives us an idea of the tunes that were current at the time in the area. Perhaps many came from the travelling fiddler, Celter, but tunes always travel, particularly good ones. Regardless of the ultimate source, what we are interested in is the body of tunes played in this particular area and those which have survived to the present day. Obviously there were other tunes which don't appear in

---
8. Pee Flanagan's *Handsome Sally,* which came to us through Cathal, has a different setting to that found in *The Gunn Book*.

the manuscript and we have evidence of this also from John McManus' playing. From his Uncle Hugh, he inherited a whole repertoire not to be found there. Some appear on the CD such as *Dickie Gossip* (a completely different tune to the standard one), *Uncle Hugh's* and *Big John's Reel*. Again from his uncle, he has *John's Hard Jig* (Cathal McConnell's title), a tune with echoes of earlier harp music, and a version of *The Blackbird*, played as an air, hornpipe and reel, along with numerous others.

The collection would appear to have a Scottish influence with titles such as *The Braes Of Auchintyre, The Ereshire Lasses, Miss Huntly's Reel, Miss Hamilton's Reel* and others. But the extent of this influence becomes more problematic on closer examination. *Miss Huntly's*, for example, is a version of *The Ewe Reel*. We would assume that a tune with the title *Lady Anne Montgomery* would be of Scottish origin, yet interestingly, Cathal McConnell, who has lived in Scotland for some thirty years and is familiar with the music scene there, is not aware of this tune having been played before it was popularised by The Boys of the Lough. Similarly with *The Loon Lasses*,[9] although the word "loon" is Scottish dialect for silly or giddy. The title *The Sprig Of Stradone* might sound Scottish, but it is a version of *Maguire's March*. (Stradone is in County Cavan, not far across the border from Derrylin.) Also there are many tunes with local names such as *The Humours Of Mackin* and *The Humours Of Swanlinbar*. This does not, of course, guarantee that they are of local origin and we can see that *The Humours Of Mackin* is a version of *The Fermoy Lasses*. All in all, what we are dealing with here is a mixed and varied local repertoire, with tunes deriving from many sources. Some may well have been composed locally, but we have no way of knowing now. Luckily, John Gunn recorded them for us and his family preserved his manuscript carefully down the years. It is a fascinating document and worthy of closer and much more detailed study.

Cyril Maguire. Courtesy of Pat Reilly, photographer, County Fermanagh.

---

9. This tune became generally known as *The Noone Lasses*. However, John McManus always knew it as *The Loon Lasses* and learned it from his Uncle Hugh.

Cathal McConnell.

CHAPTER 3
A Life on Stage
Interview with Cathal McConnell

Cathal McConnell has been with The Boys of the Lough now since 1972. They have toured the world extensively and have produced nineteen albums, a remarkable output. In addition, Cathal's solo recording, "Lough Erne's Shore", was released on cassette in 1978, and his CD, "Long Expectant Comes at Last", was launched in 2001. A summary of Fermanagh-related tunes and songs on these recordings shows how powerfully local material has influenced Cathal all his life. See table below for his recordings to date.

Songs

In Praise Of John Magee	song	John Maguire, Roslea	1973
The Old Oak Tree	song	John Maguire, Roslea	1973
Lough Erne	song	Paddy Tunney, Belleek	1973
Farewell Lovely Nancy	song	Pat Magee, Ballintra	1973
The Mountain Streams	song	Paddy Halpin and son Jimmy, Newtownbutler	1975
O'Reilly From The County Cavan	song	John Maguire, Roslea	1976
The Rushes Green	song	John and Valerie McManus, Knockninny, Derrylin	1976
Erin The Green	song	Nellie Mullarkey, Roslea	1978
Edmund On Lough Erne's Shore	song	Mick Hoy Derrygonnelly	1978
Welcoming Paddy Home	song	Willie McElroy	1986
The Leitrim Queen	song	Tommy McGovern	1987
Lovely Ann	song	Rose Johnson of Ardgart, County Fermanagh	1987
The Hills Of Donegal	song	Willie McElroy	1988
The West Of Ireland	song	Seamus and Packie McBrien, Derrylin	1999
Bellisle	song	Ed Trickett (American Folk Singer) see page 136	2001

Dance Tunes and Miscellaneous

McMahon's (The Banshee)	reel	James McMahon, Roslea	1973
The Boys Of Twenty-Five	reel	Mick Hoy, Derrygonnelly	1973
The Halting March		Tommy Gunn, Derrylin	1973
Chase Her Through The Garden	reel	Mick Hoy and Eddie Duffy	1975
Lady Anne Montgomery	reel	Tommy Gunn, Derrylin	1976
The Puck's	reel	John Joe Maguire, Kinawley	1978
The Wedding Of Molly	air	John McManus,	1978
Peter Flanagan's			1978
McHugh's Reel		Eddie Curran, Derrylin	1978
Nugent's Reel		From Sean Nugent of Ederney	1978
Big John's	reel	John McManus, Knockninny	1978
The Noone Lasses	reel	Tommy Gunn	1978
The Three-Hand Jig		Tommy Gunn (came from Francie Tummins of Tranish Island on Upper Lough Erne)	1978
Andy Kerrin's Set Dance		Andy Kerrin, Derrylin	1978
Kitty The Hare	reel	John McManus, Knockninny	1978
Big Terry McAloon's	reel	John McManus, Knockninny	1983
The Green Cockade		Tommy Gunn	1986
The New Ships Are Sailing	reel	Eddie Duffy, Derrygonnelly	1987
The One-Horned Buck	reel	Eddie Duffy, Derrygonnelly	1987
Maho Snaps	jig	Mick Hoy	1988
Big John's Hard Jig		Big John McManus, Knockninny	2001

Many of these songs and tunes have become part of the popular repertoire. *Welcoming Paddy Home,* which Cathal collected from Willie McElroy (see p. 62), has become particularly popular and has since been recorded numerous times by different artists; the same is true of *Edmund On Lough Erne's Shore* (see p. 69). Of the tunes, *Lady Anne Montgomery* and *The Loon Lasses* are the most widely known. Both tunes are in *The Gunn Book,* but Cathal heard them first from the playing of Tommy Gunn.

Cathal's major source in the Derrylin area has always been John McManus. Cathal generally calls him "Big John" and has named some of his tunes accordingly. However, at the other end of the county, around Derrygonnelly, Cathal collected from two very significant sources: Mick Hoy, a fiddle player from Cosbystown, and Eddie Duffy, a flute player. He met them for the first time in the early 1970s when Eddie was around seventy-eight years of age.

We have been very fortunate indeed that Cathal made a point of preserving all of this material. Had he not, a large number of highly unusual tunes would have been lost. It is largely because of this that the production of this book and two CDs has been possible. He has been both the main contributor and the central inspiration.

Conversation with Cathal McConnell, 23 April 2003

When did you first meet Eddie Duffy?

I met Eddie first in '71 or '72. I think he was seventy-eight years old that time. It was at some musical function, I can't remember where, and at some point he says to me, 'I have tunes that nobody knows. I'd like you to have them,' which was an honour. So we drove down one cold winter's night. We almost didn't make it because our first driver let us down, but it was lucky that we did because Eddie was waiting in his good suit. And there was a Swedish guy called Karl Jonson – he called himself, in Irish, Cathal McShane – he was there with his big tape recorder, and of course my sister Maura[10] was there as well. I think he was going to give some of that stuff to the archive, to Breandan Breathnach. I think he was going to do that. Whether he did or not, I don't know. I was excited because it was a great find of tunes, rare tunes, strange tunes, from this area – nothing I had ever heard before in my life. I think the first tune he played was *O'Connell's Reel*. He played a lot of stuff that he never played afterwards, *The Hawk Of Ballyshannon, Paudeen O'Rafferty, The Girl In Danger*. He played two versions of *The Pinch Of Snuff* – nearly the same – and *Lannigan's Ball*. It was a treasure of tunes and he started playing first. And then later on Mick came in and we played some tunes together. We made a very special tape. I set about deciphering these tunes and started playing them, but I never thought they would be popular. It was a wonderful experience and thankfully Eddie was alive for a long time after. My father died in 1974. He [Eddie] came down with a Mass card with his wife and he said, 'I'm sorry for your trouble.' And then he asked, 'Is there any chance we'd play a tune?' [*Cathal laughs at this memory*] and that

---

10. Maura, Cathal's sister, collected tunes and songs as well as noting details of dancing in Fermanagh. Her private archive has recently gone to the Irish Traditional Music Archive, Merrion Square, Dublin.

Eddie Duffy and Mick Hoy.

was the time he played *The One-Horned Buck*. He played a main body of stuff but he seemed to forget some of them later on. He obviously had prepared himself for that first occasion.

Eddie talked one time about playing at the house dances with William Carroll...

Eddie said that he [Carroll] was a wonderful loud player. There used to be a feis around that time and William Carroll would only allow one man to play with him at the feis. I think he was called Quinn. Carroll would play on his own at the house dances, and he would have a whiskey at the beginning of the night and one towards the end, but he could take plenty when the whole thing was over. Mick Hoy said that he ruined a flute one time by making the holes bigger trying to get more sound out of it. He was accounted a wonderful player and one of the last tunes that he played was *McCormick's Jig*. I think he must have died some time in the '20s and I think Eddie went to Canada in the '20s. Eddie used to play with Felix McGarvey – he was from Drumbeggan. But Carroll, even when you take away all the mythology surrounding him, seems to have been a very special player and Eddie tried to emulate his performance. It's quite a decorative way of playing. You can see it in *The Girl In Danger*. There'd be a piping influence in it, and Eddie had a lovely lightness in his playing.

And your father, Cathal, was he from Fermanagh originally?

Oh yes, my father was born in Tully in 1903 and his father was born also in Tully. My father was Sandy and his father was Sandy and then his father Mickey, who also played the flute, came with his half-

Felix McGarvey, flute player, with his wife circa 1956. Courtesy of Jim Harren, Monea, County Fermanagh.

brother, called Grumbling Barney. There were two of them, Stutterin' Mickey and Grumblin' Barney. They were evicted from a house called Cockety Hill, near Lisbellaw, and they came to Tully and they bought one of these long thatched houses divided in two and brought up their families there. My great-grandfather [Mickey] died in something like 1886 or '87 and he'd lived to be a big age, eighty-six or thereabouts, so he goes back a long way. My father played the flute and a bit on the accordion. My grandfather, whom I never knew – he died in 1932 – he played the flute and they all sang.

Sandy was well known as a local historian, wasn't he?

He was, very well known. He found a stone grid in Cleenish for making the bread and then the Belfast people said, 'You found one for Dublin; you couldn't get one for us?' So he found another. The poor creature had to carry it up all the way, and when I went there, I couldn't see the thing – packed away somewhere.

And where did he get all his folklore?

He was just interested in things – in land, in people, in customs. He was, I suppose, quite well read, although he didn't have a formal education like my mother. He loved poetry and language. He ran a shop and my mother was a teacher. Her first job was teaching on Inishmore Island on Upper Lough Erne. It was a small school and she loved it. She lodged in a local house [with] a man called Peter Dolan. She met my dad on Lough Derg. He proposed to her there. 'You'll never be more miserable than you are now,' and put a ring on her finger. They got married in 1939. She didn't play or sing, but she loved people and liked to meet different people. But the teaching, and I'm fond of teaching, runs back in her family. Her father Dinny, who died when she was seven years old, was a teacher. Then my mother was fostered out to aunts. She contracted the Asian Flu in 1918. Her sister Alice died from it. She always maintained that what saved her was goose, eating goose, which you would think would kill you.

Would your father have written down the songs that he made up?

I don't remember him writing them. He used to get my mother to write things when he was doing folklore. I don't have any of his writings, but I do have some letters of people answering him. He wrote local songs. *The Second-Hand Trousers* he adapted from another political song. *Ballyconnell Fair, The Bellanaleck Lights, The Knockninny Men* were all his, and the one about myxomatosis. He had a great sense of humour and was a great storyteller.

So did you all begin the whistle and flute at home – you never went to classes?

My father showed us the basics. Cormac dropped out early on and the flute was handed over to me and of course, I couldn't see properly at the time. I should have had glasses since I was three, I didn't get them until I was seven or eight, I don't know why. I learnt mostly on the old Clarke's C. They used to give trouble, and my father used to operate on them and break them. I would play one yet, but I don't have the affection that people often have for them.

Was it the top notes were a problem for you?

Well, they were a product of their time. They used to get quite smelly and the wood used to swell. As a kid it was a joy to me when the new Generation whistles came in.

You remember when the Generation whistles first arrived!

It was possibly some time in the late '50s. Nobody travelled in those days. It would have been some man going to Belfast and he would bring back a flute; he used to buy these D whistles in Matchetts, and he brought me this D whistle and it was a joy. Well, it was a note higher after the Clarke's; it spoke and there wasn't this sort of breathy sound and it was more true. That's probably why I've been bonded to the Generation D and probably will be for the rest of my life. The Generation D was better than the newer ones if you could get a good one – they either worked or they didn't work at all. I couldn't say for sure when they began to creep around the country but it was around that time that they first came to us. There was a man used to come around on a mineral lorry – you know, selling lemonade and all that – and he used to come in and he played the whistle. It was a céilidhing house and he used to get me to play and he maintained that I was playing the whistle in 1954. But I do have a memory that they got me a fiddle before that – my first instrument was the fiddle – and I struggled with it, but I didn't stick with it. I suppose the flute was my natural one.

Laurence Nugent (plays Eddie Duffy tunes on CD, vol. 1).

At what stage would you have picked up your first flute?

The first flute I got from a man called Owen Shannon from Tempo. It was a flute in three parts with just the one key, the E Flat, in concert pitch, I think. I played that for a while, and then the old flute I think I got from Irvinestown, from a man called Reihill. It cost a fiver.

Did he have a shop?

No, he was just someone we knew and that cost a fiver. And I think it was called a Valstaff, that was a fiver. It was fully keyed and I had it for twenty-six years.

Was that the one with the star around the embouchure?

That's the one. There's a picture in that book that Bobby Hanvey did with a big beard playing the flute; and it's that flute. In fact, I still have my great-grandfather's flute, which is an F flute, boxwood, Nicolson.

That's the man came to Bellanaleck first of all?

That's right. Mickey, or Stuttering Mickey, as he was called. I started to learn the whistle around that time from Pee Flanagan. That would have been really from observation – people learnt that time by watching.

Cathal McConnell. Courtesy of photographer Bobby Hanvey, from *Merely Players,* his publication of photographs from around Northern Ireland.

And was he a whistle player, or flute, or both?

He played the whistle. He probably played the flute in his younger days – I never saw him play it. He played the whistle very traditional, you know [*lilts*], very strong, very, very good fingers for rolling the notes and he played the fiddle way down on his chest, old style. He would have played some of the Coleman tunes and various things. I would have learnt those early tunes from Pee Flanagan.

Your Stony Steps*?*

Not that one. You know that version of *Over The Moor To Maggie* [*lilts*] and his versions of *Down The Broom, Handsome Sally, Round The World*. He learnt from his father, who was Claude (they were all small men), and he maintained that the Claude was French. There were four of them: Pee, Phil, Mac and there was Joe, and my mother told me they used to play up in Arney. They lived in a place called Ristoney. They were entertaining. Pee was also a good singer. Pee learnt me those tunes, but of course my first influence on the flute was John Joe Maguire, the Puck. I heard him some time in the '50s and was really impressed. He was from a place called Drumroosk, in Kinawley. He played a lot of McKenna. He was very into the old seventy-eights. He learnt in a flute band.

Peter Flanagan. Courtesy Henry Glassie.

Peter Flanagan (right) with his brother Joe. Courtesy Henry Glassie.

Pee's father, Claude, was a tailor and he died before I got to know them. He knew he was going to die and just went around visiting everyone. And then, of course, I met Big John some time in the '50s. I remember Hugh Gunn (John's uncle, a fiddle player). I heard them playing in our house one night. And later on I was with the céilidhe bands. There was the Harp of Erin in Derrylin. I learnt some from seventy-eights – not a lot – but I do remember Hughie Gillespie and his *Master Crowley's*.

And were you already travelling further afield at this stage?

Well, there were the céilidhe bands, and then the first fleadh I went to was in Longford in 1958.

And were you competing?

Both myself and Mickey competed that year. My father took us around to some of those, just to further us in the music I suppose. The other thing helped me was when my mother put us in for a talent competition in Bundoran and I went up and played the whistle – it would have been at that stage – and they gave out the first, second and third, and they eliminated the young fella from the North and there was an uproar.

Why were you eliminated?

Because I wasn't from Donegal. And my mother in a fit of rage wrote to the BBC in Belfast and asked could her son go up for an audition, and I went up with my little whistle and played. And as soon as I'd finished, the man in charge said, 'He's passed the audition.' What they had done was to play the tape through to Raidio Éireann – the audition was being done for the two at the one time. It might have been in Dublin, there was some woman called Cecily Matthews doing a programme called *Children at the Microphone*, and after that I started playing on the radio. I got a lot of radio exposure playing whistle and flute. By the '60s I was already quite experienced. I would need to go through hypnotism to remember all about those days. We played up in Dublin on various occasions. And then my mother took us to fleadhs more regularly, and then eventually I won the senior flute (and whistle, I think) in 1962 in Gorey. The man that had won the previous three years was Paddy Carty. It was nerve-racking. You played your tunes and then went out. You didn't hear what the other person was playing. The adjudicator was Vincent Broderick, and there was a Superintendent Doherty from Wexford.

You mentioned one time playing around parish halls. You met Ben McGrath and people like that. Do you remember?

Oh yes, we did indeed. I remember playing with another band in Enniskillen called The Devenish Band with Johnny Maguire, Phil Palmer and a few others. And we played in Arney and parish halls here and there. These were sit-down concerts – we'd be up on the stage. Then we got a guitar in and started singing around; me and Mickey and Sean.

Cathal McConnell (left) with his brother Mickey at a singing event in The Ballyhugh Arts Centre in Ballyconnell. Courtesy of Brian Mulligan, photographer, County Cavan.

And were you getting paid for these?

Not at all. We got paid nothing. And Sketch McGrath and Charlie McNally were the big names, but they probably never got a penny either. Charlie McNally was a comedian in much the same mode as Sketch. Sketch was very much the mainstay. He could turn round a bad function. He sang and told stories and so on, and there was another man from Enniskillen called Kit Cleary, who was similar.

Around '67, I began to come into contact a lot with Tommy Gunn – Jason Gunn he was known as – and he used to ask me up to play in Belfast, and playing at one of the programmes in Belfast, I met Robin. Robin was running a folk club, The Ulster Folk Music Society, and he asked me to do some work with him. So I played around Pat's Bar and places. But I used to go to Dublin also and played round the scene before it became really popular and The Castle Céilidhe Band started coming up that time. In the '60s also, I started doing some folk programmes. There was a John Whitehorn, *Sing North, Sing South*. There was Maurice Leitch at the BBC. He liked airs and he used to use me a lot on *Come Listen Here a While*. This was all BBC stuff. I was constantly up in Gunn's in Botanic Avenue.

Around '66, Peggy Seeger and Ewan McColl were playing in the Whitla Hall with Tommy Gunn, myself, and probably Sean McAloon. Then Robin, myself and Tommy Gunn were invited to do a tour of the clubs in the late '60s We didn't have a name at the time, but we did a programme and whoever

Mick Hoy. Courtesy of Colm McGuinness, photographer, County Fermanagh.

was producing it said, 'You have to have a name,' and Tommy came up with The Boys of the Lough, and that stuck. Then later I met Aly – he was playing with a man called Mike Whelan. We came together at a festival in Aberdeen and there was a suggestion that we should come together and do some gigs. Robin was doing a thesis on lunacy in the 19th century and we were all busy, so it wasn't feasible at that point. We went to America for the first time in 1972 – that was Aly Bain, Robin Morton, Dick Gaughan and myself.

Conclusion

The Boys of the Lough became hugely popular, particularly in America, where they still have a loyal audience. To commemorate twenty years on the road together, they played in Carnegie Hall and were hosted by Garrison Kieller, presenter of the famous radio programme, *Lake Woebegone Days*. They were distinctive with their mixture of Irish and Scottish (often Shetland) music, and were prolific in output. I have highlighted the Fermanagh material which they used for the purposes of this project, but all their other material, from Scotland, America, Quebec Province, Nova Scotia, Cape Breton and other places, is of equal interest.

Appendix to Chapter 3

The following was written by Séamus Ó Coinne, the well-known Derrygonnelly fiddle player. It gives an interesting overview of the music scene around Derrygonnelly down the years. He credits Jim Hoy of Cosbytown (son of fiddler Mick Hoy) for information on these musicians.

Article by Séamus Ó Coinne written for Comhaltas Ceoltóirí Éireann, Fleadh Cheoil Fhéarmánach, Sunday 14 June 1987.

There has been a strong music tradition in the Derrygonnelly area as far back as the folk memory goes. Felix McGarvey from Drumbeggan was a well-known flute player and his brother Andy sang. Felix learned to play the uilleann pipes in his later life. Another man noted for his flute playing in the area was Eddie Duffy. Eddie is now remembered in the annual Derrygonnelly Festival named after him. Felix and Eddie played great music together at house dances and parties. Alfie Brennan was a flute and whistle player *par excellence* who worked here during the '50s. Francis John McGovern, a stonemason from Kiltyclogher, is still talked about. Francis John played the whistle and flute and is remembered now by the tune known as *Francis John's*, popularised by a neighbour of his, modern-day fiddler Charlie Lennon.

William Carroll, who lived next to Drumbeggan School, had a great reputation as a flute player. He was the oldest of this group of musicians. It is said that Carroll tried out the flute in different spots in the room in which he was playing until he found the place where the sound best pleased him. One thinks of the old custom of placing the skulls of large animals under selected flagstones in old houses to amplify the beat of the solo dancers' feet on the floor. Was William Carroll using his (possible) knowledge of this custom to his advantage?

Jimmy Duffy, brother of Eddie, is still mentioned locally for his tunes on the melodeon. Elizabeth Hoy, mother of the talented Hoy family, was another melodeon player. She sang songs and lilted tunes as well. Eddie Durnien, a bus conductor around here for some time, is still remembered as the man who introduced the new B and C style of fingering on the accordion to the old "push and draw" musicians.

The name Brian Maguire needs no introduction to local musicians of this generation in our area. Brian, who lived in Meenagleeragh, was the best known and respected of the fiddlers of the old school. He was noted for his tone, attention to tuning, and generosity in commenting on those of lower calibre than himself. Brian was well known in the Boho district and played at dances there for years.

Patrick John Feely from Garrison was a noted fiddler of that era, as was John Quinn from Ballaghameehan. Pat Carty, Garrison, is remembered as the man who gave the name to the local jig, *Maho Snaps*.

Pat Love of Tabradan had a reputation as a good man behind a bow too. Johnny McGee of Dresternan played the fiddle and seems to have been the only pianist in the district.

Barney and Jimmy Farrell, father and son, played uillean pipes and fiddle respectively and tied fishing flies for a living. They lived around the Magheryhar area. Jimmy was drowned on the Erne at Portora.

Many of the local musicians joined a local band headed by John Dundas, drummer, during the céilidhe band era. The band was known by different names at different stages – The Sillies Céilidhe Band and the Knockmore Céilidhe Band were two of its titles. John Tierney and Charlie Keown, another two local men who played fiddles, joined its ranks. Packie McTeggart, accordion, Mick Hoy, Cosbystown and Charlie McLoughlin, Boho, both fiddlers, are some of the other names associated with it.

Other names that spring to mind while doing a past musicians' inventory of our own place, however casual, are John Cowan, Denis Rogers and Hugh Dolan – fiddlers all.

Mick Hoy with Father Seamus Quinn (or Séamus Ó Coinne).

Rosie Stewart.

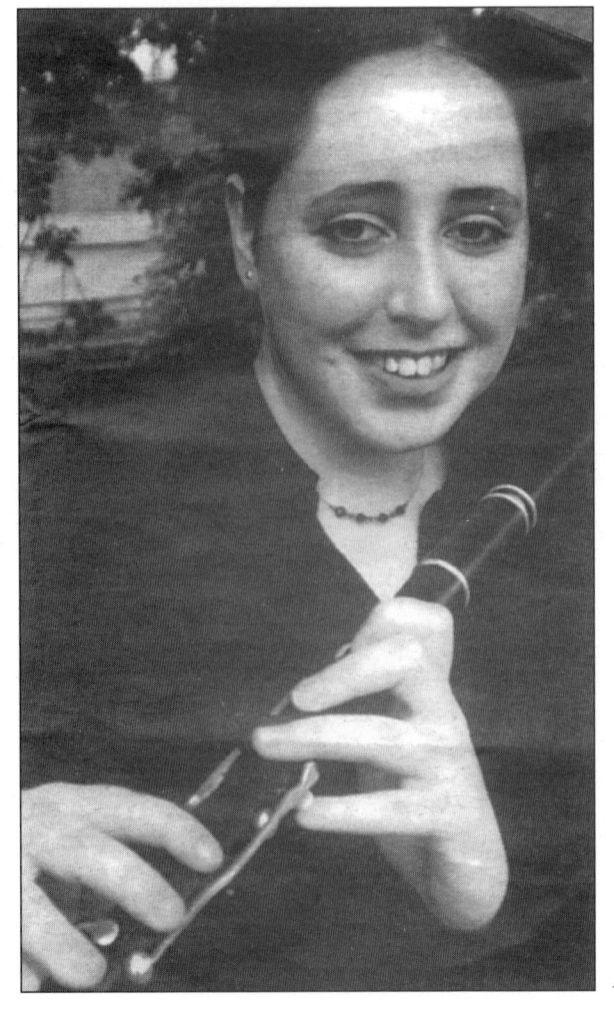

Aisling McPhillips.

Jim McGrath (left) and Charlie Woods.

Larry Hoy (left) with John Duffy, Eddie Duffy's son.

Catherine Dunne.

Below left: Ian Smith.
Below Right: Francis Rasdale.

The Assaroe Céilidhe Band. Left to right: Teresa Duffy, Larry Hoy, Padraic Daly, Seamus Sweeney (piano accordion), Charlie Lennon (double bass), Cyril Curran, John Tierney.

CHAPTER 4
Song and Verse

> I love a brave fellow who cares not for shocks,
> With strength in his arm to stiffen an ox;
> Who'd knock down a gauger or carry a still,
> Though the revenue rattled from valley to hill.[11]

This was written by the poet Peter Magennis (1818–1910) who lived at Knockmore, near Derrygonnelly. He produced a volume of poetry and two novels, *Tully Castle* and *The Ribbon Informer*, amongst other writings. He knew William Carleton and William Allingham, was a close acquaintance of Lady Wilde (Sperenza) and was highly regarded as a writer, so much so that songs are often attributed to him which he probably did not write. Two of the characters he wrote about, Gerard Howden and Dominick Noone, are still remembered in local legend (independently of any written account). Howden was a famous local distiller, also from Knockmore, who lived at the same time as Magennis (he died in 1846) and the above verse was most likely written with him in mind. In *The Prince of Distillers* he says of him:

> Then hail to young Howden, with laurel we'll crown him.
> Our friend, benefactor, the valiant and bright.
> His foe, the informer, we'll certainly drown him,
> But not in the liquor we're quaffing tonight.

Knockmore, home to Peter Magennis.

---
11. *The Still, Poems of Peter Magennis*, p. 26.

Poitín, understandably, was a favourite subject of song and verse in Fermanagh (and everywhere else it was regularly made). In Magennis' poem on Howden, we have the familiar pattern of distiller as hero and revenue, or gauger, as villain. The same was true of the poems of Padraic Burns, who was also from Derrygonnelly and lived in Drumbeggan, Monea. His long poem, *The Gauger Outwitted,* is still remembered in the area, and he wrote of the time of Gerard Howden's death:

> The harvest moon, in '48
> Saw many a 'stiller working late,
> By mountain side and lonely glen,
> The haunts of poteen-makers then.
> The people, poor from '46,
> To live devised some clever tricks,
> And from Belmore to bleak Tooraw,
> They made the "Dew" – and chanced the law.

His hero is Paudha More, another famous local distiller. Paudha had already had one of his kegs seized by the revenue and, on being surprised a second time, was determined not to lose another. In the resulting chase, we can almost follow his footsteps:

> He put the keg into a sack,
> And both were soon upon his back;
> And up the glen he swiftly ran,
> The revenue following to a man.
> Then over Leglands' craggy rocks
> He led them like a hunted fox.
>
> Along the Barrs, nor far behind,
> The hunters followed like the wind.
> At times they grasped to clutch the sack
> When Paudha was crossing Aughnaglack.
> To gain the woods he bravely strove,
> At last they reached Shillaghan grove.
> The hunters searched for hours there
> To trap their victim in his lair;
> But Paudha left the wood unseen,
> And crossed the hills to Carngreen.[12]

---

12. *The Gauger Outwitted*, Padraic Burns, from *The Ulster Singer*, pp. 12–16. This is a long poem of 128 lines in seven sections. Ben (Sketch) McGrath used to recite this sometimes at the end of a session in McKenzie's in Boho, or in the back-room of the Cosy Bar in Derygonnelly. It was always the high point of the evening.

Ben McGrath (right) with cousin Chuck.

Edward Flanagan, "The Poet of the Moy" (near Letterbreen), who was older than Magennis, although contemporary, wrote about a famous location for distilling and called it *Maguire's Hotel*. He had this to say about his song:

'In my early days this song was one of the most popular in all Fermanagh. In every public house and tent in the fairs it was sung and encored; in every shebeen house its strains echoed. At that time illicit distillation flourished, and everything associated with it possessed a charm for public interest and curiosity. An islet in the lake in Aughlis, near the Moy, was the scene of illicit distillation; a still constantly worked there.'

He gives us the names of the distillers:

> This famed habitation, the best in the nation,
> For beauty and station all people admire,
> There's not a distiller, and travel Jamaica,
> From Cork unto Egypt, can equal Maguire;
> For jovial McCabe, he's a member to trade,
> For making malt-whiskey none can him excel,
> While Connor does wait to extinguish the grate
> And bring round the heartsease in Maguire's Hotel.

And the gauger:

> When Bacchus had heard how their praises extended
> Their liquor commended and ordered therefore,
> He licensed Maguire, and all his attire,
> To keep a still-fire by island or shore;
> So you island intruders and mountain malt-brewers,
> Shut up in your caves and enclosed in your cell,
> Draw near to this island lest Willis should find you
> And your Permit get signed in Maguire's Hotel.

The battle between distiller and gauger seemed to dominate the older poems, but as poitín-making declined with changing times, we see other ways of looking at it. Robin Morton, one of the founder members of The Boys of the Lough, collected songs around Ulster in the 1960s. His most important source by far was John Maguire, a singer from Roslea. Robin wrote John's life story, *Come Day, Go Day, God Send Sunday* as told by himself (John), and included his songs (fifty-five in total) and the stories about them. One song, *Tom Kelly's Cow*, is about a farmer from the Roslea area who was a well known poitín maker. According to John Maguire, Tom kept the barrel of poitín in the byre and, on one occasion, went off sporting himself for a couple of days. The cows became thirsty and one broke loose, drank from the poitín barrel and got very drunk. The song imagines her bewailing her hangover:

> Next morning she awoke with a sad broken horn
> Cursing the day and the hour she was born
> She cursed Tom and John, Mr Beattie likewise
> And all the still-tinkers that's under the skies.

But her wiles had not deserted her:

> Oh the cow came to Tom and she whispered in his ear,
> 'You won't tell John that I got on the beer.
> If you don't, 'pon my honour with a heart and a half,
> I will bring you against Lammas a fine heifer calf.'

One day at school, the "master" and the assistant teacher kept him behind after classes and told him they had heard that he had *Tom Kelly Making The Poteen And The Cow Getting To The Barrel* and would he sing it. He was surprised but sang it and then,

> They went up and had a talk among themselves after it. They took fits of laughing at it and they come back down and each of them gave me half-crown apiece. I know I went home in good form, five bob at that time was a big thing. They were laughing hearty when I left the school.

John claimed that poitín-making was eventually brought to an end in the area, not by the police, but by the church, as too many young people had taken to drinking it.

> The bishop was far more effective. They all went by him. They didn't like the law altogether, but like they weren't as afraid of them as they were of their own clergy.

Poitín-making faded from song and verse, but people, as a subject of comment, certainly did not. John Maguire told Robin Morton of a Sergeant Neill who used to spray potatoes for people in the area. A local man called William Quigley made up a song about all the people he sprayed for:

> He sprayed for Peter Lowry and he sprayed for Larry's Hugh,
> And he turned to Greaghollia and he sprayed for Bishop Grew.
> He sprayed for Patrick Anthony and for the Widow's Pat
> And he sprayed for John The Carpenter, that wore the three-cocked hat.
>
> He sprayed for the McGrory's, that lived up at the Road,
> And he sprayed for Paddy Berry, that lives in Mullin's Cove,
> He sprayed for Tommy Armstrong, that kept the kicking mule;
> And he sprayed for decent Robert Ellett, that hopped round upon the stool.

They were more circumspect about names around Knockninny. A new ferry boat, on Upper Lough Erne, running from Knockninny to Lisnaskea (called 'Skea locally) was the subject of this song:

> There's an old maid who lives down in the valley,
> Whose name I'm not going to tell,
> She swore that she never would marry
> For men they were only a sell.
>
> But when she saw this fine boat put in motion,
> She thought she would ne'er cease to run,
> 'Til she landed below at Knockninny,
> And sailed down to 'Skea with Pat Gunn. (see p. 21 for complete text)

This comes from *Pat Gunn's Boat* and is sung by John and Valerie McManus. John's mother was Katie Gunn (this was one of her songs) and her father, Pat Red Gunn, operated this ferry boat before the bridges at Trasna Island were built. It was a row boat taking twenty-five people. It is sung on the accompanying CD by John and Valerie with their son, Pat, backing. They say it was composed by a local family called Brazil. Another songwriter from the same area was Cathal McConnell's father, Sandy McConnell. He, too, wrote about Knockninny but, for some reason, was not very impressed with the men around there.

As I went out walking a down by Knockninny,
I spied an old woman both scrawny and skinny.
She sang in a voice both discordant and tinny,
'What's gone wrong, what's gone wrong, with the Knockninny men?'

Sure their footballers do badly, they lose all their matches.
They're awful bad kicks and they're even worse catches.
And the Bellanaleck boys can run through them in batches,
'What's gone wrong, what's gone wrong, with the Knockninny men?'

And all to the air of *The Bold Fenian Men*. (see p. 151)

Another part of Fermanagh gets similar attention in *The Second-Hand Trousers I Bought In Belcoo*.

The trousers did not please.

> When the wife saw the trousers she flew in a rage,
> Saying, 'They're no wear at all for a man of your age,
> With one leg so black and the other so blue,
> Ah they'd rob a child's bottle up there in Belcoo.'

The trousers are donated as a prize in the Arney bazaar.

> Well at the bazaar shure we all had great fun,
> When the trousers went up and the rickety spun.
> In the mad tear for tickets I only got two,
> But I won back the trousers I got in Belcoo. (see page 160)

Whether or not these two songs were based on some personal experiences, his *Ballyconnell Fair,* by all accounts, was based on fact (and practically all the songs and poems mentioned here were based on real events in one way or another). In this song, two brothers lose a cow on the way to the fair. It was clearly too much for Sandy to resist.

Ballyconnell Fair

Cathal & Mickey McConnell

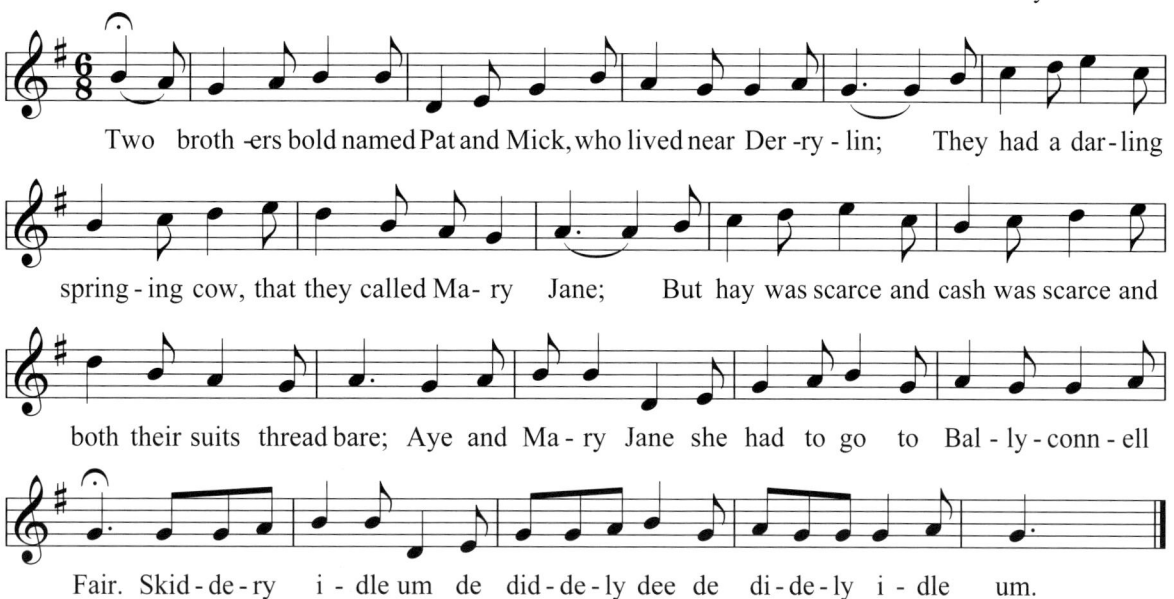

1. Two brothers bold named Pat and Mick, who lived near Derrylin,
   They had a darlin' springing cow, that they called Mary Jane;
   But hay was scarce and cash was scarce, and both their suits threadbare,
   Aye and Mary Jane she had to go to Ballyconnell Fair.
   REFRAIN: Skiddery idle um de diddely dee, de diddely idle um.

2. Now the morning of the Fair arrived, with shocking fog and mist,
   Came rowling down the hills of Doon, you couldn't see your fist;
   Says Pat to Mick, 'I'll walk in front, and you bring up the rear,
   Aye with Mary Jane betwixt us both to Ballyconnell Fair.'

3. Now at Gortaree well Mary Jane, she played an awful trick;
   She slipped into a side-road there, unknown to Pat and Mick;
   She ate a feed from Drumm's haystack, and then she made her lair,
   Aye while Pat and Mick they welted on to Ballyconnell Fair.

4. Now they reached the Green at half-past eight, approaching to daylight;
   The fog had lifted all at once, the drovers hove in sight;
   Says Pat to Mick, 'Where's Mary Jane, I can't see her nowhere?
   By the Holy Christ, it's me you drove to Ballyconnell Fair.'

5. Now both men's dead, God rest their souls, but still the story's told,
   Around the fires of Derrylin, enjoyed by young and old;
   And children ask when goin' to bed, and dashing up the stair,
   'Was it Pat drove Mick, or Mick drove Pat to Ballyconnell Fair?'

Sung by Cathal and Mickey McConnell on the accompanying CD.

In a similar vein, John and Valerie sing of the only son of a domineering mother in *The Town Of Swanlinbar*. The song, which also came from John's mother, Katie Gunn, relates some of the conversation between them.

> Oh early one morning, John with his spirits high
> Oh it's John, dearest John, you are a good boy
> Oh it's John, dearest John, you are a good boy
> But I like to see you working late and early

He cajoles enough money to go to the fair in Swanlinbar.

> Throw your mantle o'er your shoulder and come along with John
> We'll have a glass of whiskey and a verse of a song
> If your money it runs out you can call about on John
> And we'll go home drunk as Baltic in the morning

But his lot does not improve.

> It's now that I've got married and a wife for to keep
> A babe in the cradle and a babe to put to sleep
> It's outside of the door I'm scarce allowed to creep
> That's the life of a married man this morning. (see page 165)

A well-known recitation in the Derrylin area was *Maxwell's Ball*. The "ball" was in fact a house dance on Inishmore Island on Upper Lough Erne. Henry Glassie, an American folklorist, came to this part of Fermanagh in the 1970s and early '80s. He stayed there on and off over a period of seven years and put together a book called *Passing the Time*. He stayed mostly around Bellanaleck, which he called by the older name of Ballymenone. He came to rely on a small number of people as his sources, amongst them Hugh Nolan and Michael Boyle (local historians) and Pee Flanagan, the singer and musician. Michael Boyle tells the origins of this recitation:

> This Maxwell's Ball, it was in a house the name of Maxwell's in Inishmore. And of course a good deal of the lads of our country went over to it. So anyway, there was a song made. And the song was made on a girl and a fellow, do ye see. And the girl she left the fellow durin' the ball, de ye see. They were sweethearts, de ye see, and durin' the ball she left him and went away with another fellow, so he was in a terrible state, of course.

Vast numbers come from far and wide:

> They were there in all persuasions,
> In numbers great and small.

> They hailed from Carna Cara
> And from Tonyloman too,
> And from sweet old Montiagh's shores,
> Their numbers weren't few.
> They braved the dangers of the waves;
> They came both one and all
> To patronise the gathering
> That night at Maxwell's Ball.

The "ladies" are mentioned:

> The ladies they were charmin'
> And beautiful to view,
> And some were dressed in Blarney tweed,
> And more in navy blue.
> While some, they wore tight jackets
> To make their waists look small,
> Till I really thought they'd split in two
> That night at Maxwell's Ball.

The young man was "in a state" when he found that his Nora had left him. He received the customary sympathy:

> While some did laugh and more did chaff,
> While I sat in suspense
> Thinkin' how I lost my Nora
> Likewise my eighteen pence. [*The price of a cup of tea – or two?*]
> And everywhere I go, the boys do on me call:
> Or did you get your Nora
> Tonight at Maxwell's Ball?

In a more charming manner, Pheley Gunn, the poet, reflects on his predicament one morning. He was an ancestor of John McManus, and John recalls his Uncle Hugh telling the story.

> There was after being a big spree in Achlemad this night and they were all gone to bed half-drunk and whatever you like, and Pheley Gunn was a man that used to go around the country mowing with the scythe. So Pheley arrived about six o'clock in the morning and there wasn't a sinner to be seen. So he propped the scythe up on his shoulder and he says:

Ye dancers arise and open your eyes
And behold the bright rays of the sun
For there you do lie as the day passes by
And no breakfast for poor Pheley Gunn.

Annie McKenzie, right, with daughter, Eileen McGourty.

As in any area, many of the songs are part of a wider tradition. One unusual example of this is *The Frog's Wedding*, sung by Annie McKenzie of Boho (née Donegan – formerly Derrylin). Sean Corcoran collected songs in Fermanagh between 1979 and 1985 on behalf of the Arts Council of Northern Ireland. He concentrated mainly on the Derrygonnelly area and recorded from Mick Hoy (Cosbystown), Ben McGrath (Monea), Cassie Sheerin from Knockmore and Annie McKenzie from Boho, amongst others. He published *Here's a Health: Songs, Music and Stories of an Ulster Community* (cassette and booklet) in 1986. *The Frog's Wedding* is a local variant of a song which is internationally known mainly through the version by Burl Ives:

A frog went courting he did ride um-hum
A frog went courting he did ride um-hum
A frog went courting he did ride
Sword and pistol by his side um-hum

Annie's version (to a different air) begins:

There was a frog lived in a well
Fol-lie, linkum-laddy,
And a mouse that kept a mill,
Tidey-ann, tidey-ann, diderum-diedum-dandy.

One day says the frog, 'I'll go to coort,'
Fol-lie, linkum-laddy,
'With me shoes as black as soot,'
Tidey-ann, tidey-ann, diderum-diedum-dandy

He proposes in the following way:

'Arragh, Missie Mousie, will you wed?'
Fol-lie, linkum-laddy,
'Will you come into me bed?'
Tidey-ann, tidey-ann, diderum-diedum-dandy.

She cautiously replies:

'Now, Uncle Rat is not at home,'
Fol-lie, linkum-laddy,
'Without his lave I'll marry none,'
Tidey-ann, tidey-ann, diderum-diedum-dandy.

Celebrations begin, neighbours come in (ducks, kittlings and cats) and things seem to get out of hand. The song ends:

Now this whole family went to wrack,
Fol-lie, linkum-laddy,
Between kittlings, ducks and cats!
Tidey-ann, tidey-ann, diderum-diedum-dandy. (see page 143)

There are literally hundreds of versions[13] of the song to be found in England, Scotland, Ireland and America. Allegorical interpretations have been given, but John Molden, an authority on traditional song, and particularly the northern Irish songs, takes the opposing view and says that, in all likelihood, it is simply a children's song made up and sung for enjoyment. Annie first heard it when she was about nine years of age:

---

13. The song itself may be traced through four centuries. *In The Complaynt of Scotlande* (1594), [it begins] 'The frog cam to the myl dur.' From *The Oxford Dictionary of Nursery Rhymes*.

At that time there were ones from the South of Ireland came down and they were hired hands round the country, servant boys and servant girls, all hired in houses round the country. They were mostly from Leitrim, and the men were hired on the farm and the women in the houses. And then there were céilidhing houses. Everybody went to a céilidhing house you see.

And our house was what they called a céilidhing house. And this boy he used to sing – we called it *The Froggie In The Well*. We enjoyed it that much that every night he came in he had to sing it, and we picked it up. Nobody wrote anything down that time.

The Hiring Fair, the period away and return home was possibly one of the means whereby songs travelled from place to place. Another Fermanagh singer, Willie McElroy, was hired at Fivemiletown Hiring Fair. He was born in 1904 in Carrickapolin, near Roslea, but is generally associated with Brookeborough, where he did most of his singing in later years in Bernard and Attracta McGrath's pub. Cathal McConnell heard his songs early on, and recorded a number of them with The Boys of the Lough, most notably *Welcoming Poor Paddy Home*. *The Rambling Irishman* was later recorded by Dolores Keane, and three others had local connections, *The Fair Of Enniskillen, Farewell To Ballyshannon* and *Leaving Of Donegal*. Bobby Hanvey[14] came and recorded Willie in the kitchen of McGrath's pub in Brookeborough in 1977. These songs were released on vinyl through the Belfast Outlet label under the title *The Fair Of Enniskillen*. As part of this recording, Willie talks about the Hiring Fair and the farmer he worked for. It is the story of a hard life but not without a certain humour.

Willie McElroy... on the Hiring Fair:

There was the May Hiring Fair at Fivemiletown and there was the November fair. There was six months every time and I walked out to look for a bit of work and I stood until a man came forward 'til me... I was around about twenty and there was no money, no work, you had to wait 'til you got it... a man comes over and asks you, 'Are you going to work? Would you come to me for six months?' The Hiring Fair was on a Friday... 'You'll start on Monday morning. I'll give you five pounds' and before he left you he took you away and stood you a drink, a trate – he gave you two and sixpence, what they call Earnest Money, because you were bought, you couldn't go to nobody else once you got that. You got your five pounds for six months, and you were out when the stars was on the sky, and when the stars was on, you quit and you had to work like that for the five pounds.

What kind of work did you do?

Labourer, in the field and out of the field and milking and everything. You were kept and boarded.

---

14. He also published a book of photographs, *Merely Players: Portraits from Northern Ireland* (see photograph of Cathal McConnell, p.39)

And had you a decent room?

Only middling, now.

And were you well fed?

Only half-fed.

Had you any entertainment?

Well, you could go out and make that yourself once you had your day's work done.

What time did you work to?

You were up there in the morning anywhere around six, and from that to seven, and you were out there until you could hardly get out of the field. You got up in the morning and there was no fire on. Eight o'clock the creamery man got the milk and I had to have the creamery can on the stand at eight o'clock, and I ate nothing for maybe a good half-hour or maybe an hour after that, and I didn't get too much to ate now.

The man you were working for, was he hard on you?

He was, just a wee bit hard, now. He ate all himself, he gave nothing to me.

And after the six months were up?

Well, I got me money but it wasn't hard to collect for I had the weight of it lifted.

(Conversation courtesy of Outlet Recording Company Ltd, Belfast.)

A song which seems to have been almost lost from the singing repertoire was collected by RTE producer Harry Bradshaw in 1981. He has connections with Boho through his wife's family, and he took an interest in the stories local people told him about Dominick Noone, who joined the Ribbonmen in the early years of the 19th century, informed on them and for this was assassinated and thrown down a very deep pothole in the Boho Mountains, since called "Noone's Hole", although in earlier accounts it is called "The Sumera". This is one of the most enduring stories of the Derrygonnelly and Boho area and people know it (or parts of it) independently of any written accounts. Magennis wrote a number of poems about it, and Dominick Noone is the subject of his novel, *The Ribbon Informer*. In this story, he combines the local legends of Noone and Gerard Howden, the famous distiller, and says in a footnote that 'the majority of all the incidents related' are fact. (Dominick Noone was murdered in 1826, and Gerard Howden died in Enniskillen Gaol in 1846.) Some years before Peter Magennis' death, he was visited by an English journalist who contributed an article on him to an Irish journal. He, too, was struck by the Dominick Noone story and by Magennis' ballad about it:

Mr Magennis actually remembers the awful death of this picturesque character, although it took place in the reign of George IV. Dominick Noone, he tells us, was a native of Connaught. He was young, an ardent lover, a wanderer at night in the cabins among the mountains, impassioned in regard to the love of one particular female, deceived by a friend in whom he confided to further his amour. When betrayed in his hopes and disappointed in his expectations, in hatred to that friend who had deceived him he resolved on revenge, became an informer against Ribbonmen, and succeeded in transporting the man who had deceived and betrayed him. He then became a general informer against others, banished many from their homes, and for personal safety was himself placed in the prison of Enniskillen. A secret conspiracy was formed against him, and by the devices of a female whose brother or lover was imprisoned on his account, Noone was decoyed from the prison, and in female apparel made his escape to the mountains. There he lingered among the cabins, was deceived by hollow smiles and false promises, and on pretence of being married to the woman who had conveyed him from prison, he was allured to a distance at night and murdered. His remains were flung into a deep cavern, known ever since as Noone's Hole. Mr Magennis remembers the body being brought to light in the presence of the Sheriff. The Hole is hundreds of feet deep[15] but the corpse had lodged on a jutting crag. None of the murderers was discovered. Secrecy, mystery, and awe still surround the commission of this dark deed, and a thrill accompanies the narration of it in the locality where it occurred.

In his long ballad on the subject, Peter Magennis wrote:

A stranger he came in friendship's name,
With the youth of the valley to dwell –
The songs he sung, the jests he flung,
The tales he was wont to tell,
A favourite made him with old and young –
They loved the stranger well.

But sometimes a moody mind had he,
Till vanished his gloom away,
And often he walked to the mountains at eve,
Nor returned till the break of day;
When the old surmised in his bosom deep
Some solemn secret lay.

Noone came to Fermanagh some time before 1826 and '...was hired to a family called Acheson... [he] was going out with a young lady from Derrrygonnelly, supposedly an Ann Jones. Local stories tell us that Ann jilted Noone and, to get his revenge on her, he turned informer on her brother and other Ribbonmen in the district.'[16] In March 1826 a local man, John Maguire, was tried in Enniskillen and

---

15. Noone's Hole is a 350ft shaft in the Boho district in a region known locally as the Barrs – from *Dominick Noone, the Ribbon Informer*, Eileen McKenzie, *Fermanagh Herald*, 5 November 1977.
16. *Dominick Noone and How Noone's Hole near Derrygonnelly got its Name* by Breege McCusker, *Clogher Record*, 1988, p. 137

sentenced to transportation for life. When Harry Bradshaw was researching the story for RTE, he recorded Miles Doogan of Meeniclybawn, a townland close to Garrison, who sang for him the now little-known *Dominick Noone The Traitor*:

> Come all ye loyal heroes wherever you may be,
> I pray you pay attention and listen unto me;
> The more I'm on my banishment no one let us pursue,
> And here's a health to every girl that keeps her secrets true.
>
> I being a young Fermanagh man my age was scarce nineteen,
> Being full of life with my dog and gun to the caves I oft have been;
> But Dominick Noone the traitor he swore my life away,
> And that is one of the reasons why Maguire's on the sea.
>
> He swore I was leader over fifty men and more,
> And that I was a member of all the Ribbon Corps;
> The judge he rose and this did say Maguire you must go,
> And bid adieu to all your friends likewise to the Barrs of Boho.
>
> If I had my loyal counsellor O'Connell here today,
> This very day without delay would surely set me free;
> But the judge and the grand jury Noone's cause they did maintain,
> And says the prisoner at the bar must cross the raging main.
>
> Maguire being undaunted at what the judge did say,
> Without the least of fear or dread I will boldly sail away;
> But before I do discover and reach some foreign isle,
> For Edward Jones I'll make great moans likewise his sturdy child.
>
> Here's a health unto Fermanagh, likewise to the Barrs of Boho,
> The parting of my parents it grieves my heart full sore;
> But if ever I come back again I'll visit you once more,
> And I'll shake the hand of all young men that joins the Ribbon Corps.
>
> And if ever I come back again I'll visit you once more,
> And in pleasure find drinking strong wine convenient to Knockmore.

The song is from John Maguire's point of view and suggests that Ann Jones was closely involved, but whether as the original lover who jilted him, or as the girl who inveigled him out of jail and into the mountains that night, or both, is unclear. It is also unclear what happened to her afterwards. According to Breege McCusker:

Some people say that for a long time she hid in the mountains as the yeomen were looking for her. She was hidden in a turf stack and the local people brought her food. On one occasion she had to hide under water with only her mouth above. Finally she made it to the town of Enniskillen dressed as a man and from there made her escape to America.

In *The Ribbon Informer*, Magennis gives the girl who was used as the decoy to take Noone into the mountains the name of Lucy Harvey. He imagines his captors holding a mock wedding celebration before conveying him to his death. A fiddle plays; they drink poitín, dance and sing:

Nothing could exceed the pleasure of the party, and one rollicking young fellow, with winks and nods, sang the following:

I'll dance at your wedding, Dan Connolly,
I'll dance at your wedding, Dan Connolly;
If the party should make only one two or three,
I'll dance at your wedding, Dan Connolly.

Over the mountain when stars are bright,
Over the mountain in pale moonlight,
'Tis sweet with a wedding party to be,
And I'll dance at your wedding, Dan Connolly.

The sogarth he lives beyond the moor,
And soon we'll knock at his cabin door;
And then a married man you'll be,
And I'll dance at your wedding, Dan Connolly.

Three of the other songs included are of interest. *Erin The Green* was recorded live by Cathal McConnell at a singing event in the Ballyhugh Arts Centre, Ballyconnell, last April. It appears in the Robin Morton collection of John Maguire's songs, but Cathal learned it from a neighbour of John's, Nellie Mullarkey. (A different John Maguire[17] of Newtownbutler was also a major source for Cathal.) On *Erin The Green*, Robin Morton notes: 'This I think is a particularly lovely song... it seems to be a great favourite in the area, but not many seem to sing it, probably because it is a very difficult song to sing well.'[18] He goes on to say that Coolederry, mentioned in the song, is in the parish of Magheracloon.

Bessie The Beauty Of Rossinure Hill is sung by Gabriel McArdle. It is more generally known for the tune, as Mick Hoy always played it as an air, as does Cathal McConnell, who learned it from Mick. But

---

17. John recorded *The Neatly Thatched Cabin* in 1980 on *Voice of the People – Volume 20, There is a man upon the farm – Working men and women in song*. Topic TSCD670. Two other well-known Fermanagh singers, Paddy and Jimmy Halpin of Newtownbutler were on the same album, from a recording in 1977.
18. *Come Day, Go Day, God Send Sunday.* p. 172.

Gabriel McArdle.

Mick was also aware of the words and could sing a verse or two of it. Gabriel came across the full song eventually. He is now one of the very few people to sing it and this is the first recording of it. The Rossinure referred to in the song lies between Derrygonnelly and Boho, where the lover watches her 'cross Boho Mountain.' He is a weaver who strays from his loom (not the first) and plucks up the courage to address Bessie the Beauty:

> Oh darling then really please pardon my folly,
> For daring to speak as a goddess you know,
> And pity a slave that in deep melancholy,
> Who is struck down by cupid I'll tell you such woe.

But she is having none of this:

> She said then, 'Young man you must stop your intrusion
> On some other fair one perhaps you may strain
> For I here desire that you make a conclusion

> I will not be flattered I'll tell you quite plain.
> You know I'm no goddess not merely celestial,
> But a poor peasant daughter that lives near the mill.
> So banter no longer and treat me terrestrial,'
> Said Bessie the Beauty of Rossinure Hill.

She appears to have been one of a type:

> 'Ah, lovely creature, the pride of Nature!
> Did Cupid send you to the Shannon side?'

(whereto, properly enough)

> She then made answer, 'It's all romance, Sir,
> For you to flatter a simple dame;
> I'm not so stupid or duped by Cupid,
> So I defy you on me to schame.'[19]

Or, Paddy Tunney's *Sheila Nee Iyer*:

> It was by the banks of a clear flowing strame,
> That first I accosted that comely young dame,
> And in great confusion I did ask her name:
> 'Are you Flora or Aurora or the famed Queen of Tyre?'
> She answered, 'I'm neither, I'm Sheila Nee Iyer.
>
> 'Go rhyming rogue, let my flocks roam in peace,
> You won't find amongst them the famed Golden Fleece.
> The tresses of Helen, that goddess of Greece,
> Have hanked round your heart like a doll of desire
> Be off to your Spéirbhean,' said Sheila Nee Iyer.[20]

It is a big song, over six minutes long, and Gabriel McArdle, in his incomparable style, sings it unaccompanied.

Finally, there is *Edward On Lough Erne's Shore,* sung by Catherine McLaughlin (née Nugent) and accompanied by Brian McGrath. This song has long been identified with Fermanagh singing and is to be found in both the Derrygonnelly and Derrylin areas. John McManus knew it from local singers.

---

19. William Allingham An essay reprinted from *Household Words* to which Allingham contributed it without a signature on 10 Jan 1852 (No. 94). Ceol vol. 111, No.1.
20. *The Stone Fiddle. My Way to Traditional Song,* p. 117, Paddy Tunney, published by Gilbert Dalton Ltd, Dublin 1979.

Cathal learned it from Mick Hoy and recorded it in 1978 on his first solo album.[21] Gabriel McArdle learned it from Mick Hoy and recorded it on "Dog Big and Dog Little" in 1989.[22] Rita Gallagher, described by Paddy Tunney as "The Linnet of the Bluestacks" sings it on her album, "Easter Snow".[23]

It is another song of transportation:

> Each step I take by the winding river,
> Where we did wander in days of yore,
> They remind me of Edward my banished lover,
> And they make me lonesome on Lough Erne's Shore.

The final verse expresses a forlorn hope to be together again:

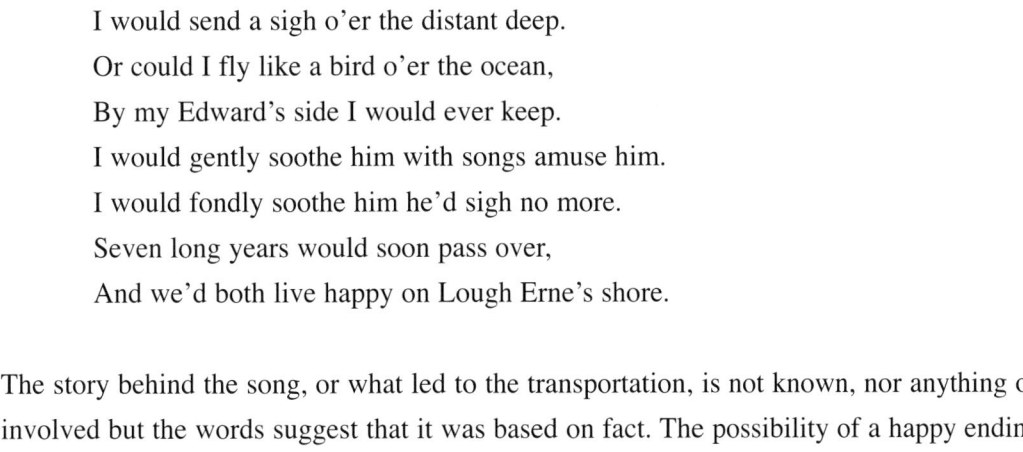

Catherine McLaughlin (née Nugent).

> Oh could I move like a moon in motion,
> I would send a sigh o'er the distant deep.
> Or could I fly like a bird o'er the ocean,
> By my Edward's side I would ever keep.
> I would gently soothe him with songs amuse him.
> I would fondly soothe him he'd sigh no more.
> Seven long years would soon pass over,
> And we'd both live happy on Lough Erne's shore.

The story behind the song, or what led to the transportation, is not known, nor anything of the people involved but the words suggest that it was based on fact. The possibility of a happy ending implied in the final verse is belied by the conditional mode of the whole. It has the ring of true emotion and is carefully crafted. The almost identical verses appear in *Poems of Peter Magennis* under the title of *Song. Air – "Youghal Harbour."*. In his preface he states that he was anxious, 'to ascertain all the legendary lore' and 'glimpses of ancient history' that he could find associated with Fermanagh. Whether the words are his own or part of that 'lore' is unclear. In it, Edward becomes 'Edmund', and later 'Edwin' on 'Lough Melvin's Shore'.

---

21. *Lough Erne's Shore,* Cathal McConnell, Topic 12TS377, 1978.
22. This album featured Ben Lennon, Séamus Quinn, Gabriel McArdle and Ciaran Curran. ceirníní cladaigh, cc51CD
23. Rita Gallagher "Easter Snow".

Mick Hoy. Courtesy of Colm McGuinness, photographer, County Fermanagh.

DANCE MUSIC & SONGS

Transcriptions by

Sharon Creasey

Tunes from *The Gunn Book* taken as found

Research: Cyril Maguire and Sharon Creasey

Notes: Sharon Creasey and Cyril Maguire

JIGS

Big John's Hard Jig

John McManus

John McManus did not have a name for this tune, so Cathal has always called it *Big John's Hard Jig*. It is a very unusual tune, and the melody and variation from the usual two parts of eight bars each suggests it may have been originally a set dance or an old harp tune. It has some similarities to *The Sprig Of Stradone*.

The Sprig of Stradone

from The Gunn Book

A version of *Maguire's March*. This tune, from *The Gunn Book*, is similar to the jig *The Rolling Waves* or *Maguire's Kick* (see O'Neill's *Music of Ireland*). There is a Stradone just over the border from Fermanagh in County Cavan. In Scotland, a "Sprig" means a tune or piece of music.

The Heart of my Kitty

from The Gunn Book

Jig

This tune, taken from *The Gunn Book* has the feel of a piping tune. It may have got this name from a song, *The Heart Of My Kitty For Me*. It is in *Ceol Rince na hÉireann Vol. 3,* and Breathnach gives the alternative titles of *Strop The Razor* and *Dan The Cobbler.*

The Humours of Glen

from The Gunn Book

Jig

Taken from *The Gunn Book,* this tune is credited by O'Neill, in *Irish Minstrels and Musicians,* to Pierce Power of Glynn, (earliest of the "Gentleman" pipers) as his song, *Plearaca an Gleanna,* composed in the early 18th century. According to O'Neill, 'It first appeared in *McLean's Scots Tunes* in 1772, and was used in O'Keefe's opera, *The Poor Soldier* in the mid-18th century. Robert Burns, with his usual ear for a good tune, used it for his *Their Groves O' Sweet Myrtle*. A florid version of the tune with eight variations was included in *McGoun's Repository of Scots and Irish Airs,* printed in Glasgow circa 1803.' Versions of this tune can be found in the O'Neill collections, *Ryan's Mammoth Collection* and many Scottish collections.

I Lost My Love and I Care Nae

from The Gunn Book

Jig

Taken from *The Gunn Book*, this tune, as with many jigs, is likely to have been based on a song. It is now usually known as *This Is My Love, Do You Like Her?* It can be found in *The Northern Fiddler* as *Kiss The Maid Behind The Byre* from John Doherty, and in *Kerr's Merry Melodies* (Glasgow, 1875) as *I Lost My Love – Scotch Jig*. In *Waifs and Strays of Gaelic Melody,* O'Neill gives it as *I Found My Love In The Morning* from the *Rice-Walsh MS,* and in the *Goodman MS* as *The Humours Of Tralee.*

Jackson's Postchaise

from The Gunn Book

Jig

From *The Gunn Book*, this is one of the many tunes composed by "Piper" Jackson of Ballingarry, County Limerick, around 1775. Further notes about the Jackson tunes from *The Gunn Book* can be found on page 29.

Jackson's Couge in the Morning

Jig   from The Gunn Book

Another of the many Jackson tunes to be found in *The Gunn Book*. As with *Jackson's Postchaise*, this tune has not been found in any other collection, although O'Neill lists it as one of Jackson's compositions in *Irish Minstrels and Musicians*. A "couge" is a porridge pot in Scots dialect.

Jackson's Babby

Jig   from The Gunn Book

From *The Gunn Book*, this tune bears a passing likeness to the tune now commonly known as *The Irish Washerwoman*, also reputed to have been composed by Jackson. O'Neill's *1,001 Gems* gives *Jackson's Delight* or *The Irishwoman* as alternative names for that tune. Although not appearing in any collections other than *The Gunn Book* under the name of *Jackson's Babby*, the tune can be found in *The Goodman Collection* as *The Rakes March* or *Bachal An Ghrina* (*The Clumsy Joker*). O'Neill's *Irish Minstrels and Musicians* lists a Jackson tune called *Jackson's Baby*. This tune can be found in Breandan Breathnach's *Ceol Rince na hÉireann 4* as *Lanamacree*, collected from the *Grier MS*, and given alternative titles of *Jackson's Babes* and *The Rose In Full Bloom*.

Jackson's Dream

Jig

from The Gunn Book

Another Jackson tune from *The Gunn Book* which has not so far been found in other collections, although it is listed by O'Neill in *Irish Minstrels and Musicians* as a Jackson composition.

The Rights of Irish

Jig

from The Gunn Book

This tune from *The Gunn Book* can also be found in The Quinn MS (1844) *as The Rights Of Irishmen*. (See page 28.) It also appears in Kerr's and Levey's collections as *The Rakes Of Irishmen*.

O Squeeze Your Thighs

from The Gunn Book

Jig

From *The Gunn Book*. This unusually-titled tune is a six-part version of *The Munster Buttermilk*. Breandan Breathnach collected a similar version from Johnny Cathcart of Derrylin in 1966 and included it in *Ceol Rince 2*. According to John McManus, Breathnach didn't actually see *The Gunn Book*. They met in John's house and Johnny Cathcart was there. In order to encourage Johnny to play, John said to him, 'I suppose you don't remember that tune,' whereupon Johnny promptly played the above. Johnny Cathcart knew John's Uncle Hugh and was familiar with a number of his tunes.

Eddie's 'Lannigan's Ball'

Eddie Duffy

Eddie Duffy had this version of *Lannigan's Ball* from William Carroll of Drumbeggan, Monea. Versions of *Lannigan's Ball* can be found in Breathnach's *Ceol Rince na hÉireann Vols. 1 & 3*, O'Neill's *1,001 Gems* and the *Petrie Collection*.

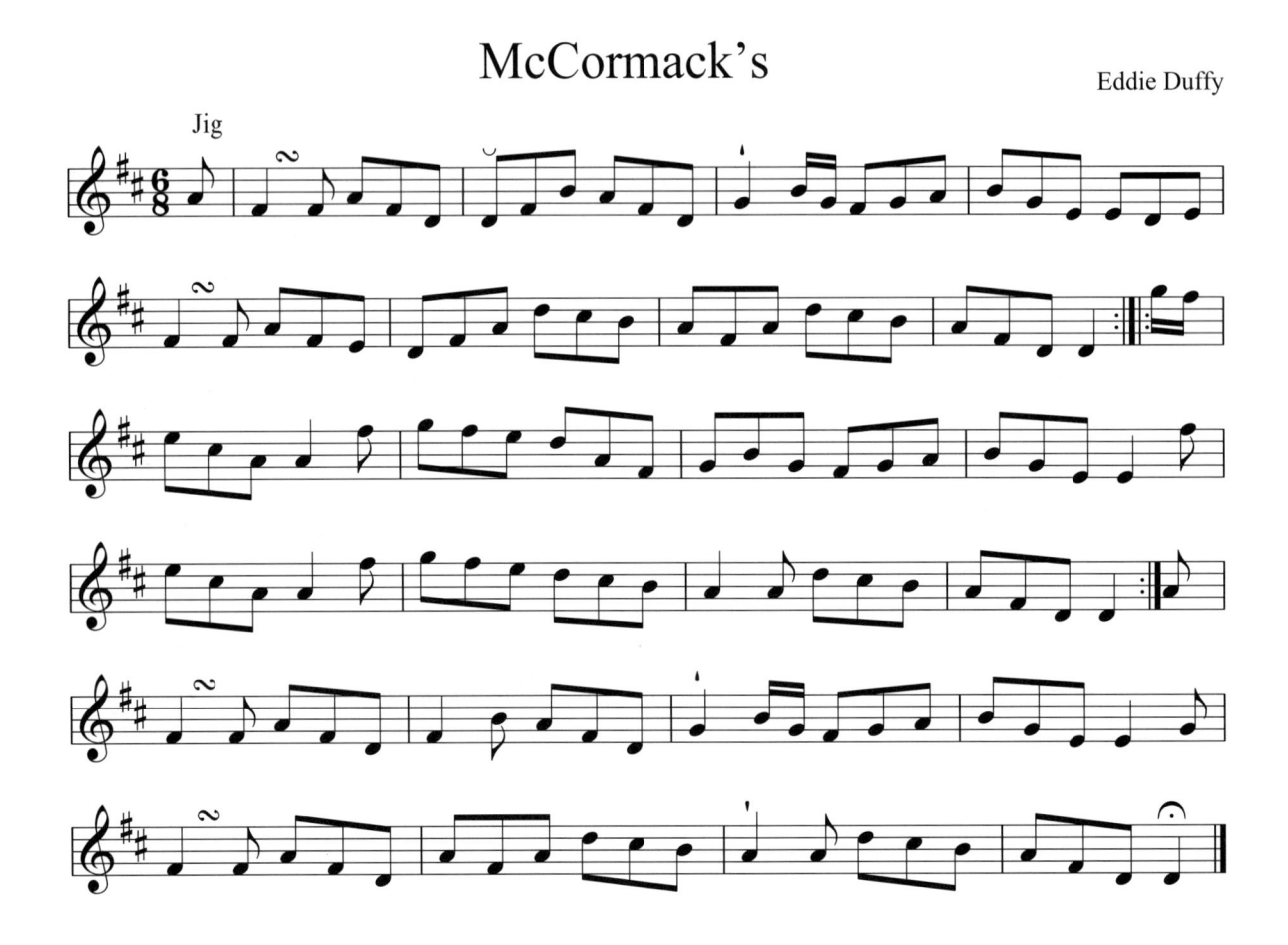

McCormack's

Eddie Duffy

From the playing of Eddie Duffy. This jig can be found on the accompanying CD, vol. 1 played by Jim McGrath and Charlie Woods.

The Mist in the Meadow

Eddie Duffy

Jig

Eddie Duffy's version of a popular local tune.

Paidin O'Rafferty

Eddie Duffy

Jig

Eddie Duffy had this unusual setting of a well-known tune from William Carroll and Felix McGarvey. *The Gunn Book* has a three-part setting of this tune. It was one of the few dance tunes to appear in Bunting's collections. Bunting collected a five-part setting from a J McCalley of Ballymoney in 1795. Five-part versions can also be found in O'Neill's *1,001 Gems* and in *The Northern Fiddler* from the playing of John Doherty It also appears in *Kerr's 1 & 2* as a two-part and three-part jig respectively. This tune is reputed to have been composed by Carolan, in honour of the boy who opened the gate at Brigid Cruise's house.

The Drumshanbo Jig

John McManus

From the playing of John McManus. This unusual jig was perhaps formerly a set dance or song.

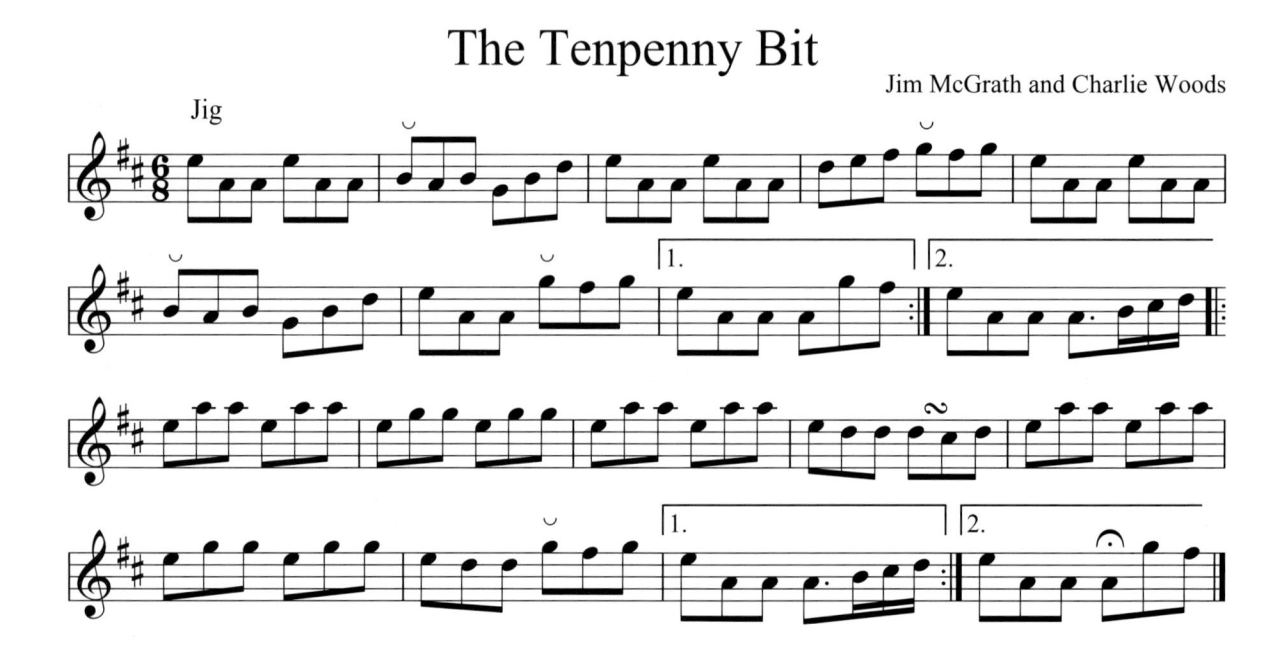

The Tenpenny Bit

Jim McGrath and Charlie Woods

This setting is taken from the playing of Jim McGrath and Charlie Woods, and can be found on CD, vol. 1. Charlie had this version from his father. There are several other different tunes which bear this name, but a version of this tune can be found in *The Gunn Book* as *The Humours Of Ballinamuck* and in O'Neill's *1,001 Gems, Ryan's Mammoth Collection* and the *Goodman MS* as *The Three Little Drummers*.

Dance Music & Songs

The High Geese in the Bog

Jig

Charlie Woods & Jim McGrath

From the playing of Jim McGrath and Charlie Woods. Charlie had this tune from his father. It is not the usual tune of *The Geese In The Bog* and has the feel of a pipe march. It can be found on the accompanying CD.

The Maho Snaps

Jig

Mick Hoy

Mick Hoy had this from fiddle player Pat Carty of Garrison, who was a policeman in Canada for a time. Pat named the tune after a particularly bumpy stretch of road alongside Lough Erne, between Enniskillen and Belleek.

James McMahon's Jig

composed by James McMahon

The Ivory Flute

composed by James McMahon

Two compositions of James McMahon, taken from Breathnach's *Ceol Rince na hÉireann 4,* who collected them from Liam Donnelly of Tyrone. James McMahon was a flute player from Roslea, County Fermanagh, and his composition *The Ivory Flute* is named after his own Drouet flute, which had an ivory head. Two further compositions, *James McMahon's Hornpipe,* and his reel, *The Banshee,* can be found elsewhere in this book.

The Lamentation of the Dead Perch

Jig — from The Gunn Book

From *The Gunn Book*. We have not been able to find a reference to this unusually-titled tune in any other collection. It has a Scottish feel to it and may well have been the air to a song, presumably a comic song.

The Top of the Hill

from The Gunn Book

This unusual tune is from the Jig section of *The Gunn Book*. The first part is in slip-jig time and the second part is a single jig. It may be an old set dance. The second part of the tune resembles the popular single jig, *Billy O'Rourke*.

REELS

Dickie Gossip

John McManus

John McManus had this reel from his Uncle Hugh. It is not the same reel as that usually known as *Dickie Gossip*. John thinks it may be of Scottish origin.

Big John's Reel

John McManus

A tune John McManus had from his Uncle Hugh and titled so by Cathal McConnell.

Uncle Hugh's

John McManus

Reel

Another reel that John McManus had from his Uncle Hugh. It is very similar to the Scots reel, *The High Road To Linton*.

The Glass of Beer

Eddie Duffy

Reel

From the playing of Eddie Duffy. Cathal McConnell had a similar version from Peter Flanagan.

The Girl in Danger

Eddie Duffy

Reel

From the playing of Eddie Duffy. (see page 35)

The Hawk of Ballyshannon

Eddie Duffy

Reel

An unusual reel from Eddie Duffy which has a Scottish sound. It came to us from Cathal McConnell. Sean Maguire had a similar tune, *The Maid Of The House*, from his father, Jack Maguire.

Dance Music & Songs

The Cocktail

Reel
Eddie Duffy

From Eddie Duffy. The first part is similar to the well-known *Dublin Reel* but with a different second part.

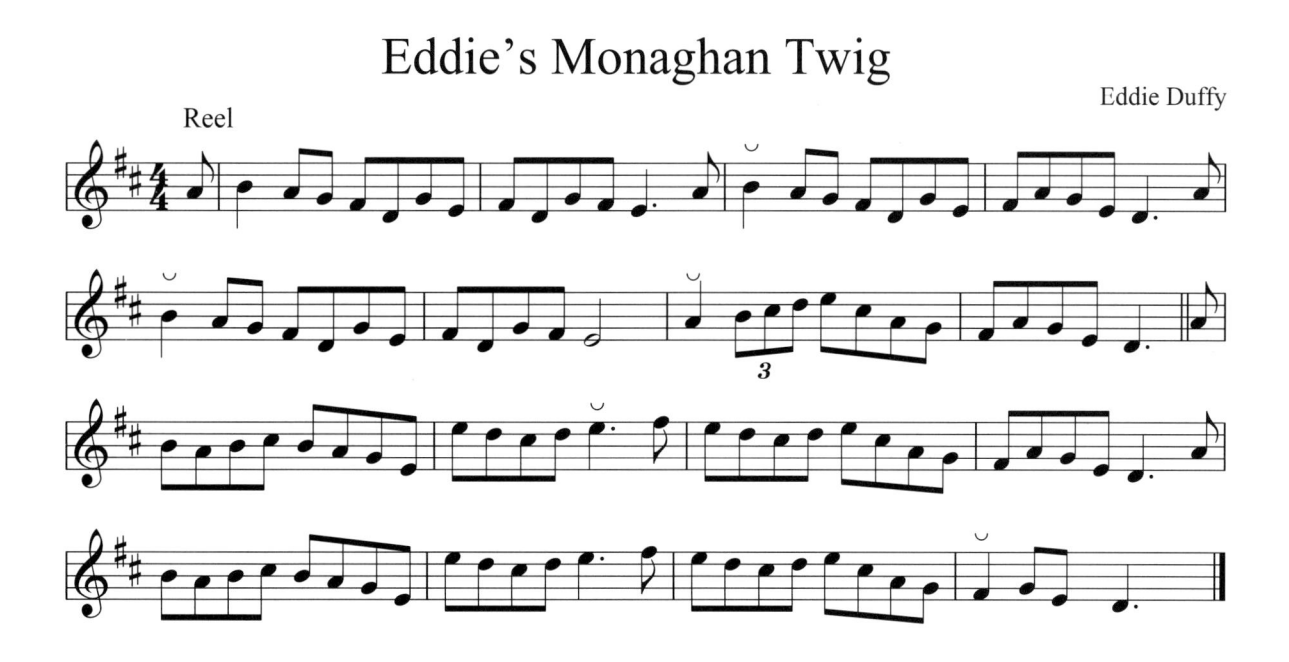

Eddie's Monaghan Twig

Reel
Eddie Duffy

Another Eddie tune from William Carroll.

The Three Scones of Boxtie

Eddie Duffy

This tune and the following are very unusual tunes from Eddie Duffy. They were generally played together.

Jig Away the Donkey

Eddie Duffy

See above. This and the previous tune gained some popularity amongst the Belfast players through Cathal McConnell.

Chase Her Through the Garden

Reel — Eddie Duffy

From the playing of Eddie Duffy.

Jig Away the Donkey

Reel — Mick Hoy

Mick Hoy learned this tune from fiddle player Andy Cassidy.

The Wise Maid
(Humours of Swanlinbar)

Reel

Eddie Duffy and Mick Hoy

Another tune from Eddie Duffy with the first part played an octave higher as the third part. See also *The Chorus Jig* (reel).

The Blackberry Blossom

Reel

Eddie Duffy

From the playing of Eddie Duffy. This tune can be found in O'Neill's *1,001 Gems* as *The New Mail-Coach*. Eddie's is a very unusual setting.

The Chorus Jig

Eddie Duffy and Mick Hoy

From the playing of Eddie Duffy and Mick Hoy. It is similar in style to another of Eddie's that he called *The Wise Maid* (also in this book). The repeating of the first part of a tune an octave up for the third part seems to have been popular even at the time of *The Gunn Book* which contains a few of these types of tunes. It is possible this practice came originally from Scotland. This reel also appears in *Ryan's Mammoth Collection* as *The Chorus Jig* and instructions for the correct dance are also given. A similar tune can be found in O'Neill's *1,001* called *The Four Courts*. Cathal McConnell sees it as a Fermanagh version of Johnny Doherty's *Glen Road To Carrick*.

Untitled Reel

Eddie Duffy

Another unusual tune from the playing of Eddie Duffy.

The Boy in the Gap

Eddie Duffy

This two-part version is from Eddie Duffy. There is a similar version in *Ceol Rince na hÉireann 3* from Matt Molloy.

The Castlebar Reel

Reel — Eddie Duffy

An Eddie Duffy tune from William Carroll. Sean Maguire had a similar version entitled *The Cow That Ate The Blanket*.

A Hard Road to Travel

Reel — Mick Hoy

From the playing of Mick Hoy. It can be found on CD, vol. 1 played by Seamus Quinn.

Stormy Saturday

Tommy Gunn

Reel

From the playing of Tommy Gunn, who had it from Francie Tummins of Tranish Island on Upper Lough Erne. (see page 27) It was named after a fierce storm which drove two of the ferry boats on the lough aground, Pat Gunn's being one of them. The tune is similar to *The Flower Of The Flock*. It is played on the accompanying CD by Brenda McCann and Cathal McConnell.

Swing Swang

Mick Hoy

Reel

From the playing of Mick Hoy.

Ryan's Rant

Mick Hoy

Reel

From the playing of Mick Hoy. This tune is similar to the first and third parts of *Granny's Gravel Walks*. The title is in *The Gunn Book*.

The Reel of Bogie

Eddie Duffy

Reel

From the playing of Eddie Duffy.

Peter Flanagan's Stony Steps

Cathal McConnell

Cathal McConnell had this setting from Peter Flanagan. He plays it on the accompanying CD.

McHugh's Reel

Cathal McConnell

Cathal McConnell had this tune from Eddie (Ned) Curran. Eddie was from Derrylin and his son Eamonn, of Monaghan, is a well-known piper. His nephew, Ciaran, plays with Altan.

The New Ships a-Sailing

Eddie Duffy and Mick Hoy

From the playing of Eddie Duffy and Mick Hoy, this tune, popular in Fermanagh, is similar to *Speed The Plough*. It can be found on the accompanying CD played as a slow and fast reel, to great effect, by Laurence Nugent.

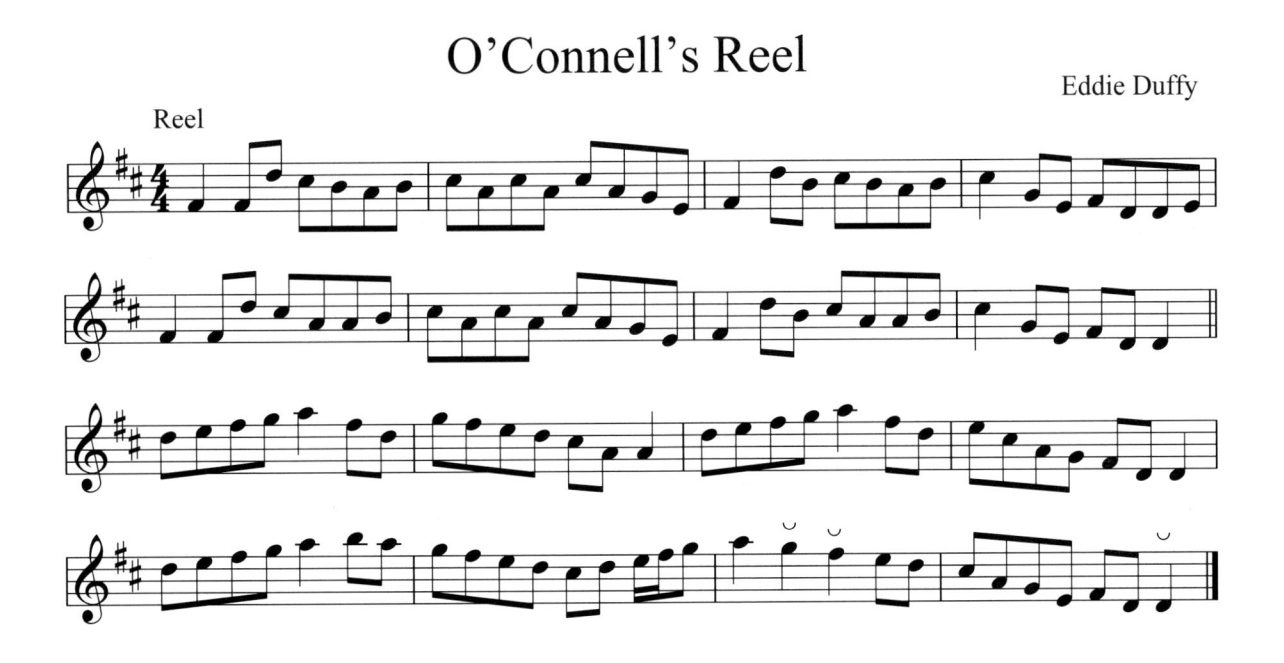

O'Connell's Reel

Eddie Duffy

From the playing of Eddie Duffy. This is one of the more unusual William Carroll tunes.

The Boys of 25

Mick Hoy

Reel

Played on the accompanying CD by Seamus Quinn and Jim McGrath, this is an Andy Cassidy tune which came from Mick Hoy.

The Banshee

Composed by James McMahon

Reel

Composed by James McMahon (see page vii). *The Banshee* is a favourite session tune wherever Irish music is played, and is often referred to as *McMahon's Favourite*. Its enduring popularity was aided by its inclusion on the first record made by The Bothy Band in 1975 on the Polydor label.

Dance Music & Songs

The Maid in the Cherry Tree
Tommy "Vetty" Maguire

Reel

From the fiddle playing of Tommy "Vetty" Maguire of Kinawley, who was recorded by Cathal McConnell back in the 1970s. O'Neill called it *The Curragh Races*. It is known locally as *The Two-Horned Buck*.

Jackson's Dairymaid
from The Gunn Book

Reel

From *The Gunn Book*. This tune does not appear in any lists of Piper Jackson's tunes, and it is possible that it is from the Jackson of Monaghan (see page 29 for more information about the Jackson tunes in *The Gunn Book*.)

The Humours of Swanlinbar

Reel
from The Gunn Book

From *The Gunn Book*. A similar version, but in the major key, was collected by Breandan Breathnach in 1965 from Mickey Doherty in Donegal. This tune is played on CD, vol. 2, by Brenda McCann.

Lady Anne Montgomery

Reel
from The Gunn Book

From *The Gunn Book*. Cathal McConnell's recording of it back in the 1970s has led to it becoming a popular session tune.

Hand Me Down the Tacklings

Reel

from The Gunn Book

One of the very unusual tunes from *The Gunn Book*. We could find no record of this tune in any other collection. It is played on CD, vol. 1 by Catherine Dunne.

The Loon Lasses

Reel

from The Gunn Book

From *The Gunn Book*. (See page 31)

The Opera Reel

Reel
from The Gunn Book

From *The Gunn Book*. The same setting can also be found in *Kerr's Merry Melodies Vol. 4* (1875) and it has more recently been recorded by De Danaan.

Handsome Sally

from The Gunn Book

Reel

From *The Gunn Book*. Breandan Breathnach had it from Mickey Doherty as *Miss Kelly's Favourite* and it is in O'Neill's *Music of Ireland* as *The New Potato*. It appears in *Ceol, vol. 111, No. 1* from the playing of Johnnie Maguire of Cavan. Cathal McConnell has the most unusual setting learned from Pee Flanagan. It is one of the few dance tunes collected by Petrie, although unnamed in his collection. It is played on CD, vol.1 by Pat McManus.

Lady Luebeck's Reel

from The Gunn Book

From *The Gunn Book*. This is the same tune as for the song *Follow Me Up To Carlow* by PJ McCall. The air is reputed to have first been performed by the pipers of Feagh MacHugh as he marched to attack Carlow in 1580:

> See the swords of Glen Imayle
> Flashing o'er the English Pale
> See all the children of the Gael
> Beneath O'Byrne's banners;
> Rooster of a fighting stock,
> Would you let a Saxon cock
> Crow out upon an Irish rock?
> Fly up and teach him manners!
>
> Curse and swear, Lord Kildare
> Feagh will do what Feagh will dare
> Now Fitzwilliam have a care
> Fallen is your star, low;
> Up with halberd, out with sword,
> On we go, for by the Lord,
> Feagh Mac Hugh has given his word;
> Follow me up to Carlow!

However, it was also published in 1775 by Scots fiddler Daniel Dow as his own composition, *Bonnie Ann*. We have not been able to find any reference to the name "Lady Luebeck".

The Milltown Lasses

from The Gunn Book

From *The Gunn Book*. We have found no reference to this tune in other collections. It is played on CD, vol. 1 by Brenda McCann.

The Poor Scholar

from The Gunn Book

Reel

From *The Gunn Book*. A lovely old version of a tune which has been often played.

Sally Kelly's Reel

from The Gunn Book

Reel

From *The Gunn Book*. The name "Sally Kelly's" appears in *The Bunting Collection* and *The Northern Fiddler*, but neither is the same tune. Played on CD, vol. 1 by Pat McManus.

Dance Music & Songs

The Primrose Girl

from The Gunn Book

Reel

From *The Gunn Book*. It is also in John McManus' repertoire.

Sir Edward Gunn's Reel

from The Gunn Book

Reel

From *The Gunn Book*. This tune, in the key of C, is similar to that now played as *Molloy's Favourite,* although the second part is completely different. We have not been able to find any other references to it. Possibly John Gunn gave it this title.

The Strawberry Banks

from The Gunn Book

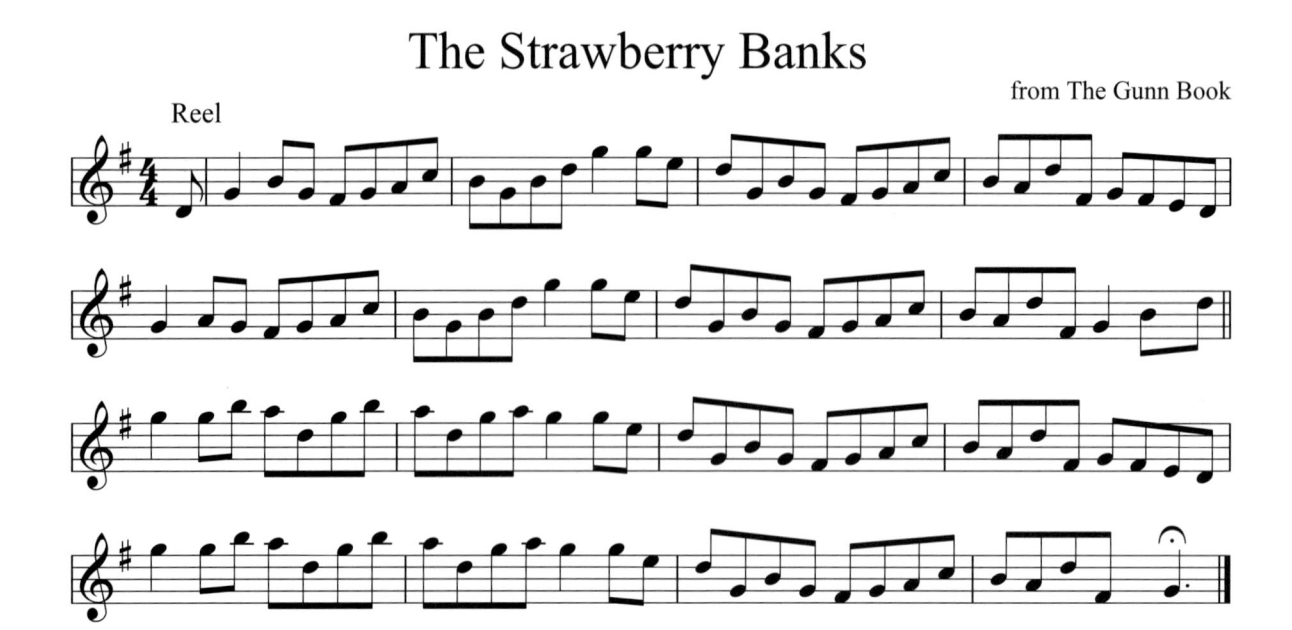

From *The Gunn Book*. This tune can also be found in the *Goodman MS* as *Betsy Baker*. John McManus has it in his repertoire.

The Rakes of Inverary

from The Gunn Book

From *The Gunn Book*. By the name and sound, this would seem to be a Scots reel, but we have not found a tune with this name in the Scottish collections.

The Humours of Mackin

from The Gunn Book

Reel

From *The Gunn Book*. It is now commonly known as *The Fermoy Lasses*. However, O'Neill gives it as *The Fermoy Lasses* or *The Humours Of Mackin*, and it is in the *Goodman MS* without a name. The local players such as John McManus know it as *The Humours Of Mackan*. It also appears in the Quinn MS (Longford, 1844) as *The Humours Of Macken*. There was a battle on Mackan Hill in 1829 (see Henry Glassie's *Passing the Time*, pp. 223–226). One man, Ignatius McManus, an ancestor of John McManus, was hanged as a result of a reprieve failing to arrive in time. Others were transported.

Miss Weatherburn's Reel

from The Gunn Book

Reel

From *The Gunn Book*. It was collected for *The Skye Collection* from the *Peter Milne Collection* as *Burn O'Cairnie,* strathspey, and also as a reel, *Miss Wedderburn's.* A two-part version can be found in *Kerr's Merry Melodies 1* as *Miss Wedderburn's Reel*.

Neils Gowan's Second Wife

from The Gunn Book

Reel

From *The Gunn Book*. This tune appears in several Scottish collections as *Neil Gow's Wife*, a strathspey, and *The Skye Collection* credits it to Duncan McIntyre. It is now commonly played as a reel, *The Watchmaker*. Eddie Duffy had a highland he called *Neils Gow's* which is similar, but not the same tune. It can be found in the Miscellaneous section of this book.

Lady Gardener's Troop Reel

from The Gunn Book

Reel

From *The Gunn Book*. This tune can be found in various collections under the alternative names *The Five-Mile Chase*, *The Four-Hand Reel*, *Lady Gardner's* and *Miss Gardiner*. It was published in *The Skye Collection* as *Mrs Garden Of Troup*, strathspey, by Robert Petrie. It is played on the accompanying CD by Brenda McCann.

The Aberdeen Lasses

Reel

from The Gunn Book

From *The Gunn Book*. Usually called *The Game Of Love,*, this tune was collected by Breandan Breathnach in 1966 from Peter O'Loughlin. Peter Browne, in his sleeve notes for the album "Jackie Daly & Seamus Creagh", notes that it is also called *Caunheen's Reel* after Mickey "Caunheen" O'Connell, a piper from Macroom, who lived around 1840.

The Bonny Boys of Ballintra

Reel

from The Gunn Book

From *The Gunn Book*. This tune appears in *The Skye Collection* as *The Lasses Of Ballantrae* in the key of F. It is in O'Neill's *1,001 Gems* as *Kiss Your Partner*. Ballantrae is on the west coast of Scotland, near Stranraer.

The Braes of Auchintyre

from The Gunn Book

Reel

From *The Gunn Book*. This fine tune is in Scott Skinner's *Harp and Claymore* as *The Braes Of Auchtertyre* – an admired old air by Crockat and in *The Skye Collection* as *The Braes Of Auchtertyre, Reel* – this majestic tune is also very effective played as a strathspey. It is still occasionally played as both reel and strathspey, usually in its earlier key of C.

The Collegians of Glasgow

from The Gunn Book

Reel

From *The Gunn Book*. As the name suggests, this is a Scottish reel, and can be found in *The Fraser Collection* as *Druimuachder* or *The Highland Road To Inverness* – pipe reel, dance and song. Cathal McConnell had it from Peter Flanagan. John McManus also plays it and it seems to have popular in the Derrylin area.

The Ereshire Lasses

Reel

from The Gunn Book

From *The Gunn Book*. "Ereshire" is an alternative old spelling of "Ayrshire". It can be found in *The Skye Collection* as *The Ayrshire Lasses – strathspey by the Earl of Eglinton*". John McManus plays this tune, but has no name for it. It is played on CD, vol. 1 by Pat McManus and Brenda McCann.

The Grand Spy

Reel

from The Gunn Book

From *The Gunn Book*. This four-part reel can be found in *The Skye Collection* as *Rothiemurchie's Rant*, a four-part strathspey in the key of C. It was also known as *Grant's Strathspey* which probably led to its corruption as *The Grand Spy*. As a further corruption of this, it is now usually called *The Graf Spee*.

Greg's Pipes

Reel

from The Gunn Book

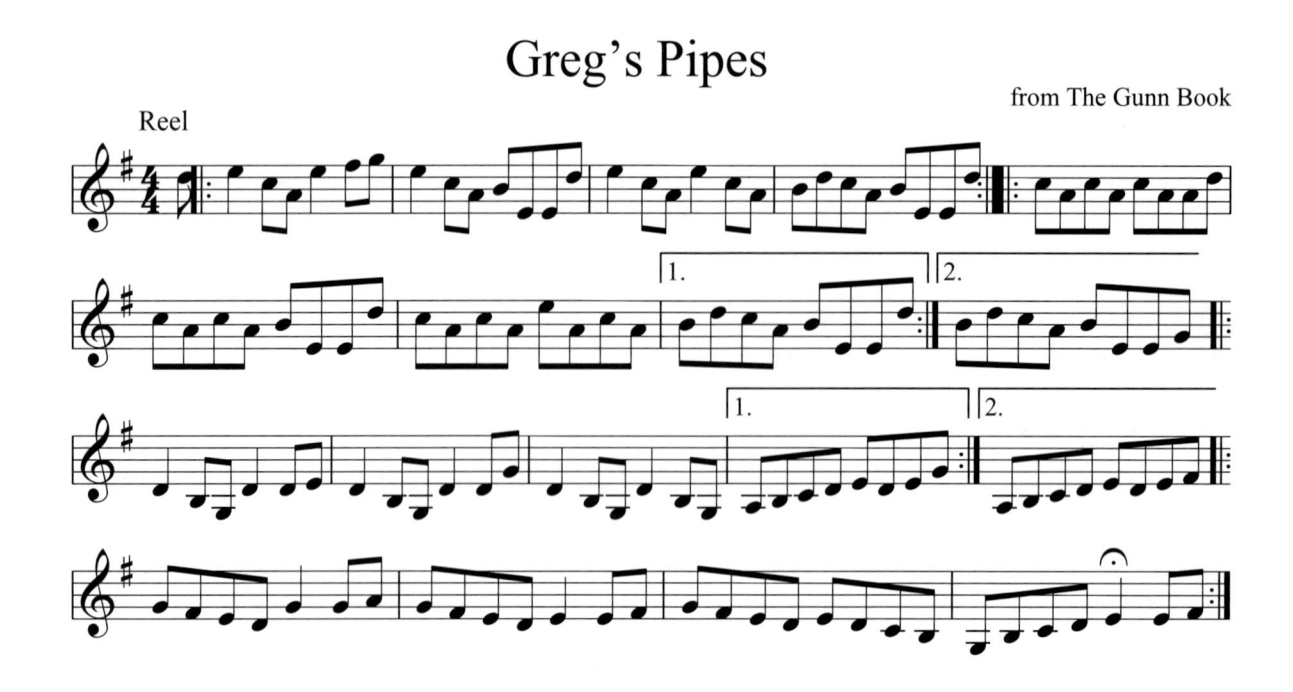

From *The Gunn Book*. A similar four-part version can be found in *The Skye Collection,* but stays in the same key (A minor) throughout. This variation could have come from *Neil Gow's Complete Repository* of 1805, where *scordatura* fiddle tuning (EAEA) is given, which would give the key change in the third and fourth parts. It has been suggested that this tune and its variations became the basis of *The Bucks Of Oranmore, The Foxhunters* and *The Reel Of Tulloch.* It was composed by Joshua Campbell, who published it in 1779 in his *Newest and Best Reels*.

Hetty's Wishes

Reel

from The Gunn Book

From *The Gunn Book*. It appears in the O'Neill collections as variously, *The Five-Leafed Clover* and *The Heel Of The Hunt*. It is a popular session tune and is now usually called *The Hunter's Purse*.

The Humours of Loughrea

from The Gunn Book

Reel

From *The Gunn Book.* Breandan Breathnach collected this from Johnny Maguire in Belfast in 1966 as *The Gossan That Beat His Father* (see *Ceol, vol. 111, No. 1),* a name that Cathal McConnell has for this tune from Peter Flanagan.

HORNPIPES

Eddie Duffy's Hornpipe

Cathal McConnell

From the playing of Cathal McConnell.

Untitled Hornpipe

Eddie Duffy

From the playing of Eddie Duffy.

The Fisher's Hornpipe

Eddie Duffy

From the playing of Eddie Duffy.

James McMahon's Hornpipe

Composed by James McMahon

James McMahon was a flute player from Roslea, County Fermanagh. Other compositions of his to be found in this book are the reel *The Banshee* and two jigs, *James McMahon's Jig* and *The Ivory Flute*. This hornpipe came to us from the playing of Brian Sutherland, fiddle player from Newcastle, County Down.

Paddy McGurn's Hornpipe

Paddy McGurn

An unusual hornpipe which Seamus Quinn learned from Paddy McGurn of Boho, County Fermanagh. This tune was recorded on the album "Dog Big and Dog Little".

Brown's Hornpipe

from The Gunn Book

From *The Gunn Book*. We were unable to find any tunes with this name in the various collections.

The Duke of Brunswick's Hornpipe

from The Gunn Book

From *The Gunn Book*. We could not find this tune in any other collections. It is, however, almost the same as the French-Canadian reel, *The Mare (La Mer)*.

Leyeer's Hornpipe

from The Gunn Book

From *The Gunn Book*. We have not been able to find any other reference to a tune of this name.

Miss Adams's Hornpipe

from The Gunn Book

From *The Gunn Book*. Also found in *The William Campbell Collection,* 1790–1817.

Miss Lacey's Hornpipe

from The Gunn Book

From *The Gunn Book*. As with many hornpipes in this manuscript, we have not found any other references to a tune of this name.

Dance Music & Songs

MISCELLANEOUS

Jimmy Duffy's Barn Dances

1.

2.

Jimmy Duffy was Eddie Duffy's brother and a much-respected melodeon player. The barn dance is performed by couples. The transcription of these tunes was taken from "Dog Big and Dog Little".

Uncle Hugh's Polka

Polka

John McManus

Taken from the playing of John McManus, who had it from his Uncle Hugh. Although John calls it a Polka, and it is in 2/4 time, it appears to be a dance or set dance tune.

The Corratistune Rose

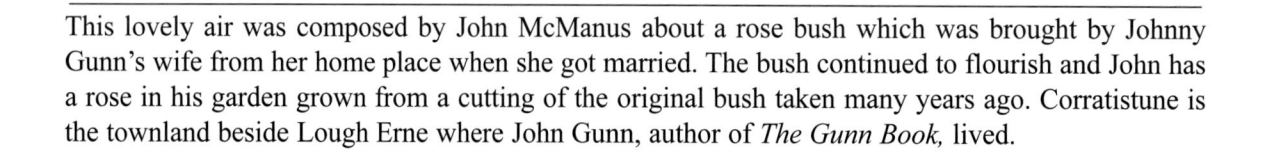

Slow Air

composed by John McManus

This lovely air was composed by John McManus about a rose bush which was brought by Johnny Gunn's wife from her home place when she got married. The bush continued to flourish and John has a rose in his garden grown from a cutting of the original bush taken many years ago. Corratistune is the townland beside Lough Erne where John Gunn, author of *The Gunn Book,* lived.

Dance Music & Songs

Katie's Lilt
John McManus

March tempo

John McManus learned this tune from the lilting of his mother, Katie Gunn. She lilted at the house dances with her brother Hugh on fiddle. It is certainly not the easiest of tunes to lilt. The fact that it was her favourite indicates her ability.

Neil Gow's
Eddie Duffy and Mick Hoy

Highland

A highland, as played by Eddie Duffy. It was also collected as an untitled highland from John Doherty for *The Northern Fiddler*. See also the reel, *Neils Gow's Second Wife*.

Untitled Highland

Cathal McConnell and Eddie Duffy

Cathal had this unnamed tune from Eddie Duffy and he feels it is of Scots origin. As with many highlands, it is probably based on a strathspey.

Green Grow the Rashes

Mick Hoy

From the playing of Mick Hoy. An unusual setting of an old, well-known tune which was used by Robert Burns for his song.

Dance Music & Songs

The Blue Ribbon

Mick Hoy and Eddie Duffy

Fling/Reel

[sheet music]

From the playing of Mick Hoy. Mick plays it at a tempo between a fling and a reel. It is common in Scotland as a fling named *Orange And Blue* or *Brochan Lom*.

Fermanagh Quickstep

from Kerr's Fourth Collection of Merrie Melodies, 1875

Jig

[sheet music]

From *Kerr's Merry Melodies,* Glasgow 1875.

Bobby Treacey's Barn Dance

Charlie Woods

Sunny Banks Highland

Charlie Woods

The first tune comes from Bobby Treacy, fiddle player from Boho, who now lives in Enniskillen. Charlie Woods learned *The Sunny Banks Highland* from his father, a fiddle player from Trillick, County Tyrone. It is a version of the reel by the same name.

Waltz

Francis Rasdale

From whistle player Francis Rasdale of Boho.

The Fairy Waltz
(Hugh Crawford's)

Cathal McConnell

Waltz

Cathal McConnell learned this tune many years ago from Hugh Crawford, a fiddler from Florencecourt, County Fermanagh.

Sandy McConnell's

Waltz

Cathal McConnell had this from his father, Sandy. (see page 55)

The Valetta Waltz

Waltz

A Jimmy Duffy waltz remembered by Jim McGrath. Tommy Gunn played the same tune in the key of G. John McManus is familiar with it. It was played for the once popular ballroom dance, "The Valetta".

The Wedding of Mary

John McManus

Slow Air

A beautiful air for a song, the words of which have been lost. Played for us one day on Iniscorkish Island by John McManus and Cathal McConnell.

The Wedding of Molly

Slow Air

John McManus

A further air, again from the playing of John McManus and Cathal McConnell.

The Blackbird

Air

Slow

John McManus

Hornpipe

Reel

John McManus had this setting of *The Blackbird* from his Uncle Hugh. He said, 'This set was used as a form of code during the time of the Redcoats: the air was played when the Redcoats were arriving, the hornpipe when they were preparing to leave, and the reel when they were away.' The words of *The Royal Blackbird* fit this version of the air perfectly.

The Royal Blackbird

On a fair summer's morning, on soft recreation
I heard a fair lady a making great moan
With sighing and sobbing and sad lamentation
And saying, 'My Blackbird most royal has flown
My thoughts they deceive me, reflections do grieve me
And I'm o'er burdened with sad misery
Yet if death it should blind me, as true love inclines me
My Blackbird I'll seek out wherever he be

'Once in fair England my Blackbird did flourish
He was the chief flower that in it did spring
Prime ladies of honour his person did nourish
Because that he was the true son of a king
But his false fortune which still is uncertain
Has caused his parting between him and me
His name I'll advance in Spain and France
And I'll seek out my Blackbird wherever he be.

'The birds of the forest they all met together
The turtle was chosen to dwell with the dove
And I am resolved in fair or foul weather
In winter or spring for to seek out my love
He is all my treasure, my joy and my pleasure
And truly my love, for my heart follows thee
He is constant and kind, and courageous of mind
All bliss to my blackbird wherever he be.'

Sean O'Boyle and Peter Kennedy recorded Paddy Tunney with his mother Brigid, and her brother Michael Gallagher, in 1952. Paddy put down the above song version of *The Blackbird* on that occasion (FOLKTRAX-163).

SONGS
The Banks of Kilrea

Gabriel McArdle

One evening for my recreation, as I strolled by the lovely mossy Bann; A young couple were in conversation, whichABrought me there for to stand; A young lad discoursing with his darling, he invited her kindly away; But she says, 'I cannot leave me parents, all alone on the banks of Kilrea.'

1. One evening for my recreation, as I strolled by the lovely mossy Bann;
   A young couple were in conversation, which brought me there for to stand;
   A young lad discoursing with his darling, he invited her kindly away;
   But she says, 'I cannot leave me parents, all alone on the banks of Kilrea.'

2. Well he says, 'Love, you are one of the fairest, and me heart you have wounded full sore;
   Come and we'll leave this land of oppression, and ould Ireland we'll never see more;
   And if you'll consent to go with me, your passage I'm able for to pay;
   And we'll reap the fruits of our labours, far away from the banks of Kilrea.'

3. Oh he says, 'Love, now don't you remember, the promise that you made unto me?
   For it being in the month of November, we were talking of crossing the sea;
   You said if you leave that you'd mourn, and invited me awhile for to stay;
   And that when the spring it returns, we would both leave the banks of Kilrea.'

4. So it's now to conclude and to finish, and I must now lay down my pen;
   Here's a health to the bonny Bann Water, likewise the fair maids round Bridge End;
   Farewell to my friends and companions, for 'tis now that I'm a-going away;
   And you'll ne'er see my face, no nay never, all alone on the banks of Kilrea.

From Gabriel McArdle, who first heard it from Len Graham and Joe Holmes. Kilrea is a village beside the Bann Water in County Derry. It was also collected by Sam Henry in 1926 from Mary McHugh, aged ninety-six, of Rasharkin, who had learned it in 1845 from a friend in Cushendall. There is a second version (also 1926) to the same tune, in Sam Henry's *Songs of the People,* but this time with a happy ending.

The Banks of the Clyde

Gabriel McArdle

Verse 1

1. As I went a-walking, one pleasant summer's evening; Down by the banks of a clear winding stream; In ambush I lay, as two lovers they were a-talking; And clearly the streams they did gently flow.

Verses 2 - 8

2. A young sailor standing by, he appeared like a stranger And he said, 'Gentle fair one, I have come from afar; But don't be afraid, or consider it a danger; To walk by the side of a jolly young tar'.

---

1. As I went a-walking, one pleasant summer's evening,
   Down by the banks of a clear winding stream;
   In ambush I lay, as two lovers they were a-talking;
   And clearly the streams they did gently flow.

2. A young sailor standing by, he appeared like a stranger,
   And he said, 'Gentle fair one, I have come from afar;
   But don't be afraid, or consider it a danger,
   To walk by the side of a jolly young tar.'

3. 'Well indeed then, kind sir, for to tell you quite plainly,
   the clothes that you wear, they are dear to my heart;
   For they're like my young William's, that I love so dearly,
   Who's crossing the ocean, to some foreign part.'

4. 'And what if your William, that you love so dearly,
   Is now joined in wedlock, in some foreign clime?
   And if that be the case, you have lost him forever,
   So here's to me your young man, and say you'll be mine.'

5. 'The flowers they will decay, in the cold stormy weather,
   And spring's gentle breezes, they then will renew;
   But this heart from my bosom, no rifle shall sever;
   So farewell my young man, I must bid you adieu.'

6. Well he paused and he gazed, with an eye full of pleasure,
   And the former disguise, well he could no longer hide;
   Till at last he explained, and joy being a measure,
   Is the smile of Jane, that I met on the Clyde.

7. For Jane she was to me, since she seemed not to know me;
   And out of his pocket, a small bill he drew;
   Saying, 'Here's fifty pounds, as a token I'll give you,
   Since you in my absence has proved loyal and true.'

8. And since that kind fortune has bought us together,
   Tomorrow my darling I will make you my bride,
   And we like two lovers, we'll never be parted.'
   And I wed with my Jane, that I met on the Clyde.

Gabriel learned this song from John Reihill of Inishcorkish Island, Lough Erne. John had it from his mother, who was from the north of England. It can also be found in *Songs of the People* collected from Frank Kealy, fiddler of Ballysally, Coleraine. Gabriel sings it on the CD "Natural Bridge", Clolar Connachta C1CD 139. Rosie Stewart also sings this and learned it from Cassie Sheerin of Knockmore.

Bessie the Beauty of Rossinure Hill

Gabriel McArdle

Slowly and freely

[Musical notation with lyrics: By the Riv-er Nam-ny, in the bright sum-mer sea-son; Where the weath-er was fine and the mea-dows in bloom; The small birds sang quiet-ly, and ev'-ry-thing pleas-ant; Which coaxed me for to wan-der, a-way from my loom. I care-less-ly strayed, by a lone-ly plan-ta-tion; For to view a fair one, some time I stood still; And she e-quals bright Flor-a, in her loft-y stat-ion; And she's Bess-ie the beau-ty of Ross-in-ure Hill.]

1. By the River Namny, in the bright summer season,
   Where the weather was fine, and the meadows in bloom;
   The small birds sang quietly, and ev'rything pleasant;
   Which coaxed me for to wander away from my loom.
   I carelessly strayed by a lonely plantation,
   For to view a fair one, some time I stood still;
   And she equals Flora, in her lofty station;
   And she's Bessie the beauty of Rossinure Hill.

2. With most admiration I did gaze upon Bessie;
   Her eyes were as bright as the dew on the rind;
   Queen Ellen was never as handsome or pretty,
   As she when she wandered down by the wood side.
   But I eagerly longed to gain conversation,
   With that matchless fair one, that had me in thrall;
   And I courteously bowed, with great humiliation,
   And I spoke to Miss Bessie from Rossinure Hill.

3. 'Oh darlin', then really, please pardon my folly,
   For darin' to speak to a goddess you know,
   And pity a slave that's in deep melancholy,
   And is struck down by Cupid, I'll tell you such woe.
   Your glancin' appearance has my heart attracted;
   You may kill or curse me, but I'm here at your will;
   This killin' affection has me most distracted,
   Miss Bessie my beauty from Rossinure Hill.'

4. She said then, 'Young man, you must stop your intrusion;
   On some other fair one perhaps you may strain;
   For I here desire, that you make a conclusion,
   I will not be flattered, I'll tell you quite plain.
   You know I'm no goddess, not nearly celestial,
   But a poor peasant's daughter, that lives near the mill;
   So banter no longer, and treat me terrestrial,'
   Says Bessie the beauty of Rossinure Hill.

5. I said then, 'Fair maiden, I am no deceiver,
   And the words I express are the thoughts of my mind;
   And for to be candid, I am only a weaver,
   Though in future life, I will be constant and kind.
   I seek your affection, I care not for money,
   That glittering trash, it cannot coax my will;
   My heart's near your bosom, accept it my honey,
   My Bessie, and beauty, from Rossinure Hill.'

6. Well she said then, 'Young man, you do speak with sound reason,
   And I cannot slight you at all for bein' poor,
   And I'm happy since poverty it is not high treason,
   For wealth unto anyone, is never secure.
   'Til I see my parents, I can give you no answer,
   Though I wish evermore my commands they'll fulfil,
   And to proceed further is only romancing,'
   Said Bessie the beauty of Rossinure Hill.

7. I bid her goodbye, and I parted with Bessie;
   I watched her cross Boho mountain, an enchanted place;
   And the most hardened tyrant I'm sure would me pity,
   If he was aware of my heart-wrenchin' case.
   So now I'll go home and apply to my shuttle;
   I'll use my exertions, my heart and my skill;
   And unto blind Cupid, I mean to do battle,
   For he wounded me sore, on Rossinure Hill.

Gabriel's rendition of this song can be found on the accompanying CD. He first heard Mick Hoy sing a fragment in the early 1970s – Mick used to play it on the fiddle as a beautiful slow air, which captivated Gabriel, but he could never find the whole song. One day in the 1970s when he was in Derrygonnelly socialising, a young boy came up and thrust a sheaf of papers in his hand saying, 'My father said to give you this.' On looking at the papers, he discovered the full handwritten version of this song. Gabriel went to look for the boy, but he had vanished. He still does not know who the boy, or his father, was. Rossinure Hill is between Knockmore and Boho (pronounced Bo) Mountain.

The Bloomin' Bright Star of Bellisle

Cathal McConnell

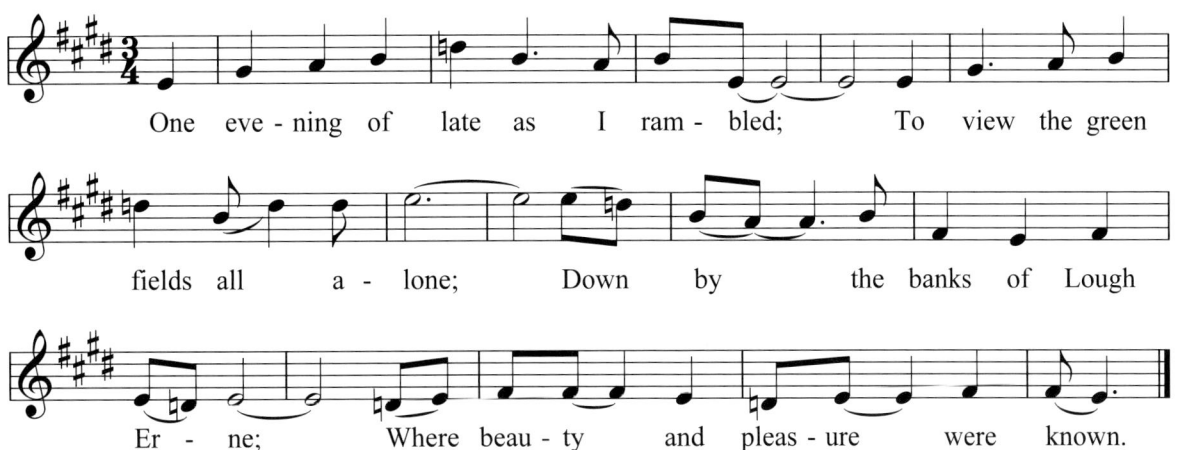

1. One evening of late as I rambled,
   To view the green fields all alone,
   Down by the banks of Lough Erne,
   Where beauty and pleasure were known.

2. 'Twas there I espied a fair female,
   She caused me to stay for a while;
   I thought her the goddess of beauty,
   Oh the bloomin' bright star of Bellisle.

3. I humbled myself to her beauty,
   'Fair maiden, where do you belong?
   Or are you from the heavens descended,
   Abounding in Cupid's fair tongue.'

4. 'Young man I will tell you a secret;
   I am a young maid that is poor;
   And to part from my joy and my promise,
   Is more than my heart can endure.

5. 'Therefore I'll remain at my labour,
   And through all the hardship and toil;
   And I'll wait on the lad that has left me,
   All alone on the banks of Bellisle.'

6. 'Fair maiden, I wish not to banter,
   I own I came here in disguise;
   I came to fulfill a last promise,
   And hoped to give you a surprise.

7. 'I own you're the maid I love dearly,
   You bein' in my heart all the while,
   For me there is no other damsel
   Than the bloomin' bright star of Bellisle.'

8. So now this young couple gets married,
   In wedlock they both joined in hand;
   May the great God in heaven protect them,
   And give them long life in the land.

9. May the great God in heaven protect them,
   And loyalty be theirs all the while,
   And honey to sweeten their comfort;
   Oh that bloomin' bright star of Bellisle.

Cathal learned this song from a recording by American folk singer Ed Trickett; it had been collected in Newfoundland in 1952 and although there is supposed to be a Bellisle in Canada, Cathal maintains that the song refers to Bellisle in County Fermanagh, near Lisbellaw, where his mother came from.

A further complication is the mention of St John, a town in Canada. There is no town in Ireland of that name. John Moulden wrote a long article for the *Canadian Journal of Traditional Music (1986)* entitled, *The Blooming Bright Star of Belle Isle: American Native or Irish Immigrant*. In it he traces three early versions of the song, one of them from Hugh Tracey of Boho. He concludes that as St John, in Canada, was one of the main destinations of emigrants from the northern and western ports, such as Derry and Sligo, that this is most likely a Fermanagh emigrant song.

To be found on Cathal's solo CD "Long Expectant Comes at Last" on Compass Records.

The Bonny Green Tree

Eileen McGurk

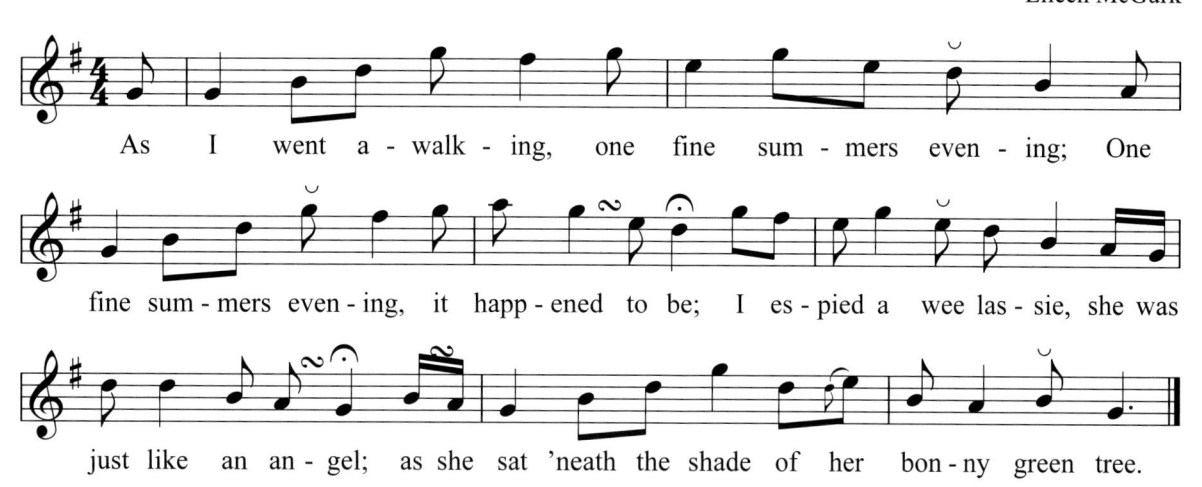

1. As I went a-walking, one fine summer's evening;
   One fine summer's evening it happened to be;
   I espied a wee lassie, she was just like an angel,
   As she sat 'neath the shade of her bonny green tree.

2. I stepped up beside her, in hopes for to view her;
   I said, 'My wee lassie, do you fancy me?
   I will make you my bride of a high rank and honour,
   If you'll shelter me under your bonny green tree.'

3. 'Kind Sir,' she made answer, 'I am not a lady,
   But a poor man's daughter of a low degree;
   Your friends would be angry and would call me a ruffian,
   If you dared for to wed a poor girl like me.'

4. 'My friends and relations, I care nothing for them,
   My friends and relations care nothing for me;
   But by this time tomorrow, my bride I will make you;
   If you'll shelter me under your bonny green tree.'

5. They both fell asleep, in each other's arms,
   Talking of love and of their wedding day;
   But when she awoke, there was no-one beside her;
   None but the shade of her bonny green tree.

6. So come all you young maidens, and pray take a warning;
   Don't pay any heed, what a young man might say;
   For when he's received the first flower in your garden,
   He'll leave you alone, just as my love left me.

From the singing of Eileen McGourty, Annie McKenzie's daughter. Colm O'Lochlainn collected this song in Wicklow from May Finnegan in 1950 for *More Irish Street Ballads*. It had previously been published in Hughes & Campbell's *Uladh* in 1904. This song also appears in the "Songs of the People", collected from Jim Carmichael, fiddler, of Ballymena in 1939.

Dominick Noone the Traitor

as sung by Myles Doogan

1. Come all you loyal heroes, wherever you may be;
   I pray you pay attention, and listen unto me;
   The more I'm on my banishment, no-one let us pursue;
   And here's a health to ev'ry girl, that keeps her secrets true.

2. I being a young Fermanagh man, my age was scarce nineteen;
   Being full of life with my dog and gun, to the caves I oft have been;
   But Dominick Noone the traitor, he swore my life away,
   And that is one of the reasons why Maguire's on the sea.

3. He swore I was the leader over fifty men and more,
   And that I was a member of all the Ribbon Corps;
   The judge he rose and this did say, 'Maguire, you must go,
   And bid adieu to all your friends, likewise to the Barrs of Boho.'

4. If I had my loyal counsellor O'Connell here today,
   This very day without delay, would surely set me free;
   But the judge and the grand jury, Noone's cause they did maintain,
   And says, 'That prisoner at the bar, must cross the raging main.'

5. Maguire being undaunted, at what the judge did say,
   Without the least of fear or dread, I will boldly sail away;
   But before I do discover and reach some foreign isle,
   For Edward Jones I'll make great moans likewise his sturdy child.

6. Here's a health unto Fermanagh, likewise to the Barrs of Boho,
   The parting of my parents, it grieves my heart full sore;
   But if ever I come back again, I'll visit you once more,
   And I'll shake the hand of all young men, that joins the Ribbon Corps.

7. TO LAST 2 LINES OF TUNE:
   And if ever I come back again, I'll visit you once more,
   And in pleasure find drinking strong wine, convenient to Knockmore.

From the singing of Myles Doogan of Garrison. For the story behind this song, see page 65.

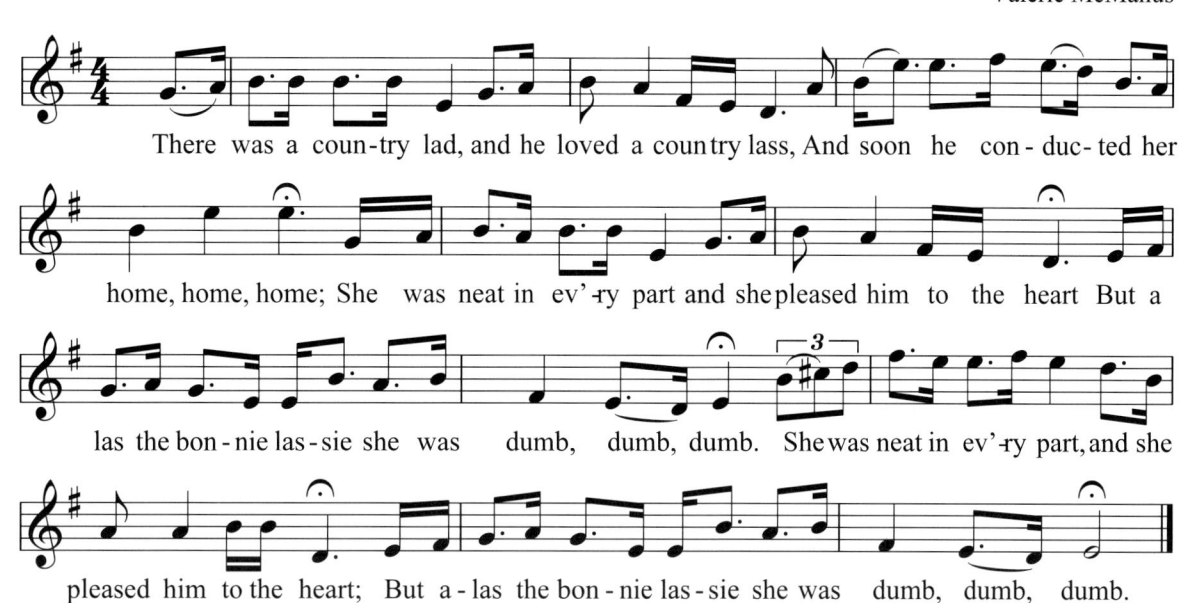

Dumb, Dumb, Dumb

Valerie McManus

There was a country lad, and he loved a country lass, And soon he conducted her home, home, home; She was neat in ev'ry part and she pleased him to the heart But alas the bonnie lassie she was dumb, dumb, dumb. She was neat in ev'ry part, and she pleased him to the heart; But alas the bonnie lassie she was dumb, dumb, dumb.

1. There was a country lad, and he loved a country lass,
   And soon he conducted her home, home, home;
   She was neat in ev'ry part, and she pleased him to the heart,
   But alas the bonnie lassie she was dumb, dumb, dumb.
   (repeat lines 3 and 4)

2. To the doctor he did her bring, for to cut her chattin' string;
   To give liberty enough to her tongue, tongue, tongue;
   When her feet began to walk, sure her tongue began to talk,
   Just the same as if she never had been dumb, dumb, dumb.
   (repeat lines 3 and 4)

3. 'Tis after that he went, with his woeful lament,
   Sayin' 'Doctor, dear doctor, what have you done, done, done?
   For me wife has turned to scold, and her tongue she cannot hold;
   I'd give any amount of money to have her dumb, dumb, dumb.'
   (repeat lines 3 and 4)

4. 'When first I undertook, for to make your wife speak,
   'Twas not an easy task that was done, done, done;
   It's beyond the art of man, you may try all the means you can,
   To make a scolding woman hold her tongue, tongue, tongue.'
   (repeat lines 3 and 4)

5. 'I'd advise you as a friend, to return home again,
   Cut a stout little hazel so strong, strong, strong;
   And anoint her jacket round, 'till you hear her ribs all sound,
   And I grant you bonnie laddie, she'll be dumb, dumb, dumb.'
   (repeat lines 3 and 4)

Sung by Valerie McManus, who learned it from Katie Gunn. It is a very old song, the conclusion of which would now not be deemed politically correct.

Edward on Lough Erne's Shore

Cathal McConnell

Slowly and freely

Oh the sun was setting behind the mountain, The dew was falling behind the lea; As I was seated beside a fountain, A feathered songster sang from each tree; With love and bliss each note was blending; Made me reminded of days of yore; When in a bower I plucked a flower, and dreamt of Edward on Lough Erne's shore.

1. Oh the sun was setting, behind the mountain,
   The dew was falling behind the lea;
   As I was seated beside a fountain,
   A feathered songster sang from each tree;
   With love and bliss each note was blending,
   Made me reminded of days of yore;
   When in a bower I plucked a flower,
   And dreamt of Edward on Lough Erne's shore.

2. A crop of sorrow my heart is reaping,
   My rose is faded and my hopes decayed;
   Since in the night-time, when all are sleeping,
   Awake I'm weeping 'til the break of day;
   Delight has fled me, and woe has wed me;
   Why did you leave me, my love astore;
   For law compelled him, and banished Edward,
   Who'd not forsake me on Lough Erne's shore.

3. The cuckoo's notes in the air are sounding,
   They appeal to feelings and please the ear,
   And ev'ry note with a bliss abounding,
   Within these valleys if he were here;
   Each step I take by the winding river,
   Where we have wandered in days of yore;
   Reminds me of Edward, my banished lover,
   And makes me lonely on Lough Erne's shore.

4. Oh could I move like a moon in motion,
   I'd send a sigh o'er the distant deep
   Or could I fly like a bird o'er the ocean,
   By my Edward's side I would ever keep;
   I'd fondly soothe him, with songs amuse him,
   I'd gently soothe him and he'd sigh no more,
   And seven long years would soon pass over,
   And we'd both live happy on Lough Erne's shore.

Cathal learned this song from the late Mick Hoy of Derrygonnelly. The tune is a variant of the song *Boulavogue*. Cathal recorded this on the album "Cathal McConnell on Lough Erne's Shore". A version of this song can be found on "Dog Big and Dog Little" by Gabriel McArdle. It can also be found sung by Catherine Nugent on the accompanying CD.

Erin the Green

Cathal McConnell

1. Draw near each young lover, lend ear to my ditty,
   That is my sad mournful tale;
   Come join me in concert, you lend to me your pity,
   Whilst I my misfortune bewail.
   The grief of my poor heart, no tongue can disclose;
   My cheeks are now pale, that once bloomed like the rose;
   And it's all for a young man, who I do suppose,
   Is now far from sweet Erin the Green.

2. It's when we were children, we walked out together,
   Along the green valleys so neat;
   And although we were childish, we loved one another,
   Whilst plucking the wild berry sweet.
   It was in sweet Arvy, we both went to school,
   He was first in his class, and correct in each rule;
   And I cheerfully walked home, through sweet Kilnacoole,
   With the flower of sweet Erin the Green.

3. His head on my bosom, he used to repose it,
   Each evening all under the shade;
   And a song in my praises, my darling composed it
   And styled me the Coolederry Maid.
   The night that I denied him, I'd die for his sake;
   It was little I thought my denial he'd take;
   Ah but to my misfortune, I made a mistake,
   When he left me in Erin the Green.

4. Oh it's little I thought that my darling would leave me,
   No matter what I'd say or do;
   For he oft-times told me he ne'er would deceive me,
   But vowed to be constant and true.
   But I need not blame him for breaking these laws,
   For to my misfortune I myself was the cause;
   And his truth and his loyalty will gain him applause,
   When he left me in Erin the Green.

5. So come all you pretty fair maids of this dear Irish nation,
   I pray you'll be steady and wise;
   And likewise give air to my kind assertation,
   And never your true love despise.
   For such foolish folly, distracted I live;
   There is no peace for me but yon dark silent grave;
   And all hopes denied me, I'll soon take my leave,
   Of the flower of sweet Erin the Green.

Cathal learned this from Nellie Mullarkey of Roslea. In *Come Day, Go Day, God Send Sunday.* Robin Morton has a very similar version from John Maguire, also of Roslea. Robin says, 'I wonder is this from the same pen as *The Maid Of Magheracloon.* Certainly the theme and style are very close.' He adds, 'The tune, by the way, owes much to the one that usually carries that great song, *The Green Linnet.*'

The Frog's Wedding

Annie McKenzie

There was a frog lived in a well; Fol aye link-um lad-die; And a mouse that kept a mill; Ti-dy Ann Ti-dy Ann; Did-der-um di-dum dan-dy

1. There was a frog lived in a well;
   Fol aye linkum laddie;
   And a mouse that kept a mill.
   Tidy Ann, Tidy Ann; Didderum di dum dandy

2. One day says the frog 'I'll go to coort;'
   Fol aye linkum laddie;
   'With me shoes as black as soot.'
   Tidy Ann, Tidy Ann; Didderum di dum dandy.

3. The horse he rode was a big black snail;
   Fol aye linkum laddie;
   Saddle and bridle in under his tail.
   Tidy Ann, Tidy Ann; Didderum di dum dandy

4. Frog rode up to Mousie's hole;
   Fol aye linkum laddie;
   Rapped the door, stout and bold.
   Tidy Ann, Tidy Ann; Didderum di dum dandy.

5. 'Ah Missy Mousie are you in?'
   Fol aye linkum laddie;
   'Yes I am, I sit and spin.'
   Tidy Ann, Tidy Ann; Didderum di dum dandy.

6. 'Ah Missy Mousie will you wed?'
   Fol aye linkum laddie;
   'Will you come into me bed?'
   Tidy Ann, Tidy Ann; Didderum di dum dandy.

7. 'Now Uncle Ratty's not at home;'
   Fol aye linkum laddie;
   'Without his leave I'll marry none.'
   Tidy Ann, Tidy Ann; Didderum di dum dandy.

8. Uncle Ratty then came down;
   Fol aye linkum laddie;
   In his silk and muslin gown;
   Tidy Ann, Tidy Ann; Didderum di dum dandy.

9. 'Bring in the table till we dine;'
   Fol aye linkum laddie;
   'Change the board and bring in wine;'
   Tidy Ann, Tidy Ann; Didderum di dum dandy

10. Just as the talk was getting slack;
    Fol aye linkum laddie;
    In walked the kittling with the cat;
    Tidy Ann, Tidy Ann; Didderum di dum dandy.

11. Cat caught Uncle by the crown;
    Fol aye linkum laddie;
    Kittling knocked wee Mousie down;
    Tidy Ann, Tidy Ann; Didderum di dum dandy.

12. Horsie snail rode up the wall;
    Fol aye linkum laddie;
    Says, 'The Devil's among you all;'
    Tidy Ann, Tidy Ann; Didderum di dum dandy.

13. Froggie then rode round the room;
    Fol aye linkum laddie;
    Just like any sporting groom;
    Tidy Ann, Tidy Ann; Didderum di dum dandy.

14. In walked a flock of neighbour's ducks;
    Fol aye linkum laddie;
    Soon devoured the bachelors up;
    Tidy Ann, Tidy Ann; Didderum di dum dandy.

15. Now this whole family went to wrack;
    Fol aye linkum laddie;
    Between kittlings, ducks and cats;
    Tidy Ann, Tidy Ann; Didderum di dum dandy

Annie McKenzie learned this song as a child in the 1940s. Dating back to at least the 16th century, versions of this popular children's song have been collected from all over Britain, Ireland and North America.

Green-Robed Inisfail

Cathal McConnell

Slow and steady

Far, far a-way from Er-in's shore, some of our brave sons roam; A-cross the broad At-lan-tic, three thou-sand miles from home; And no mat-ter where they chance to stray, they love each glen and vale; Where the Shan-non's pur-ple tide rolls free, through Green-Robed In-is-fail.

1. Far, far away from Erin's home some of our brave sons roam,
   Across the broad Atlantic foam, three thousand miles from home.
   No matter where they chance to stray they love each green and vale
   Where the Shannon's purple tide rolls free through Green-Robed Inisfail.

2. No wonder they would love their land, the land Saint Patrick blessed.
   Ah, a lovely land and God's command, the Eden of the west.
   Where peace had reigned triumphantly till the English o'er came,
   And tore our Irish homesteads through Green-Robed Inisfail.

3. When Donal sailed away from the lovely western shore
   Unto the olive groves of Spain for to return no more,
   He is gone, he is gone, our heroes cried, his loss we will bewail.
   He is gone, he's gone, he'll never return through Green-Robed Inisfail.

4. When Allen, Larkin, and O'Brien stood on the gallows tree
   Far from their homes and friends and their mother country,
   It was in that dark and dreary cell in a cold Manchester jail,
   They roared, 'May God save Ireland and Green-Robed Inisfail.'

5. Dear land you have raised another son, the best that was ever seen
   Who fought his way and routed the troops of England's Virgin Queen,
   Who fought for peace and liberty, it was dauntless Hugh O'Neill,
   Who tore their flags, their English flags, through Green-Robed Inisfail.

6. Dear land you have suffered sorely through centuries it is true,
   But thanks to God, those tyrants could not our sons subdue.
   On many a well-contested plain, where the bullets flew like hail,
   Our gallant sons, they nobly fought for Green-Robed Inisfail.

Cathal McConnell had this song, as a fragment, from Peter Flanagan. The full text is in Henry Glassie's *Passing the Time* (p. 84) where only the words are recorded. It has a fine air which, fortunately, Cathal remembered.

The Groves of Boho

Cathal McConnell

[Musical notation in 6/8 time, key of G major, with lyrics underlaid:]

When I was young my life was glad, round Sil-lies' groves and streams; Each mo-ment was a spark-ling joy, and ev'-ry day a dream; O ma-ny's the hap-py hour was spent, while yet the sun was low; Just list'-ning to the lin-net's song, that charms the groves of Boho.

1. When I was young my life was glad, round Sillies' groves and streams;
   Each moment was a sparkling joy, and ev'ry day a dream;
   O many's the happy hour was spent, while yet the sun was low,
   Just list'ning to the linnet's song, that charms the groves of Boho.

2. I knew the mavis of Monea and the blackbird of Stratore,
   The leveroc of Carngreen and the goldfinch of Knockmore;
   But of all the birds in bush or sky, that sang there long ago,
   None can compere with the linnet fair, that charms the groves of Boho.

3. I knew a white-washed cabin there, alongside Carngreen;
   I knew a red-haired colleen fair, as bright as morning beam,
   I knew one hundred thousand joys, that o'er my day will flow,
   As the lovely little linnet's song makes glad the groves of Boho.

4. Wander east or wander west, or wander far or near,
   The lovely little linnet's song, is pleasing in my ear;
   Still calling, calling, calling, 'Why do you wander so?
   Why leave these happy, happy woods, come back, come back to Boho.'

5. So now please God I'll bundle up and cut a stout blackthorn;
   The rising sun will meet me down the road tomorrow morn;
   'Farewell,' I'll cry, I'll weep and sigh, for me now guile and woe;
   'Tis wealth I'll seek in a foreign clime, as the linnet sings in Boho.'

Like *Willie Rambler* this song was well known around Boho and Derrygonnelly and was sung by Ben McGrath, amongst others.

I Have Travelled This Country

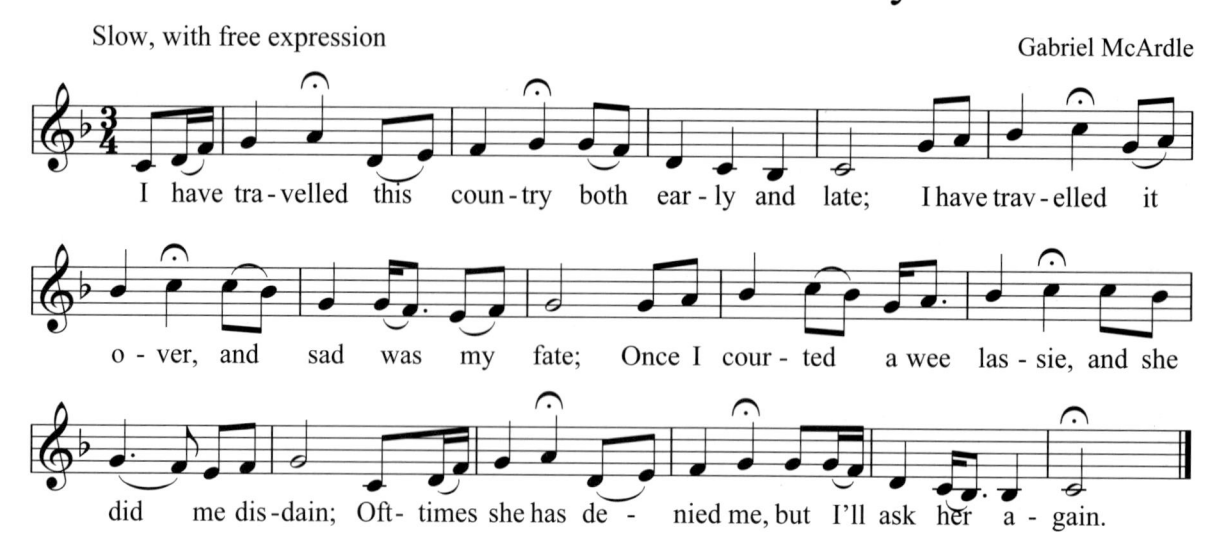

Slow, with free expression

Gabriel McArdle

1. I have travelled this country, both early and late;
   I have travelled it over, and sad was my fate;
   Once I courted a wee lassie, and she did me disdain;
   Oft-times she has denied me, but I'll ask her again.

2. Oh young Molly she was handsome, and not very tall;
   But her modest behaviour was nicer than all;
   And I'm told that she's engaged now, and cannot get free;
   She has too many sweethearts, by far to love me.

3. 'Your parents are rich, love, and you're hard to please,
   And I'll have you take pity, on a hardworking slave,
   And I'll have you leave father, and mother also,
   And through this wide wide world with your darling boy go.'

4. 'Oh Johnny, lovely Johnny, that advice never will do,
   For to leave my own country, and go along with you;
   My friends and companions, they would mourn for my sake,
   If I left my own country, all to follow a rake.'

5. 'Well if that be the case, love, my course I will steer;
   To some foreign country, without dread or fear;
   And since you'll not marry me, or with me comply,
   May the stormy wide ocean, separate you and I.'

6. Farewell lovely Ireland, and merry may you be;
   And I'll oft-times get lonesome, when I think of thee;
   And when I'm out working, on a fine summer's day,
   I will think of you Ireland, although far away.

Gabriel collected this song from Mrs Kate McHugh of Kinawley. Originally from Aughakillymaude, Derrylin, she used to sing this song with her mother in unison. This seemed to have been a common practice until relatively recently. Ben McGrath's sisters, Janie and Alice, sang in similar fashion. Best known for this are Dolores Keane's aunts, Sara and Rita.

The Illustrious Sons of Erin's Isle

Cathal McConnell

Slow

[Musical notation with lyrics: "One pleasant sum-mer's morn-ing, my mind being free from grief and care; While on a bank of sham-rocks, I sat a-while to take the air; A mai-den clad in green and gold, a bloom-ing beau-ty with a smile; Stepped up and ask-ed, 'Who are those, who gained such fame for Er-in's_ Isle?'"]

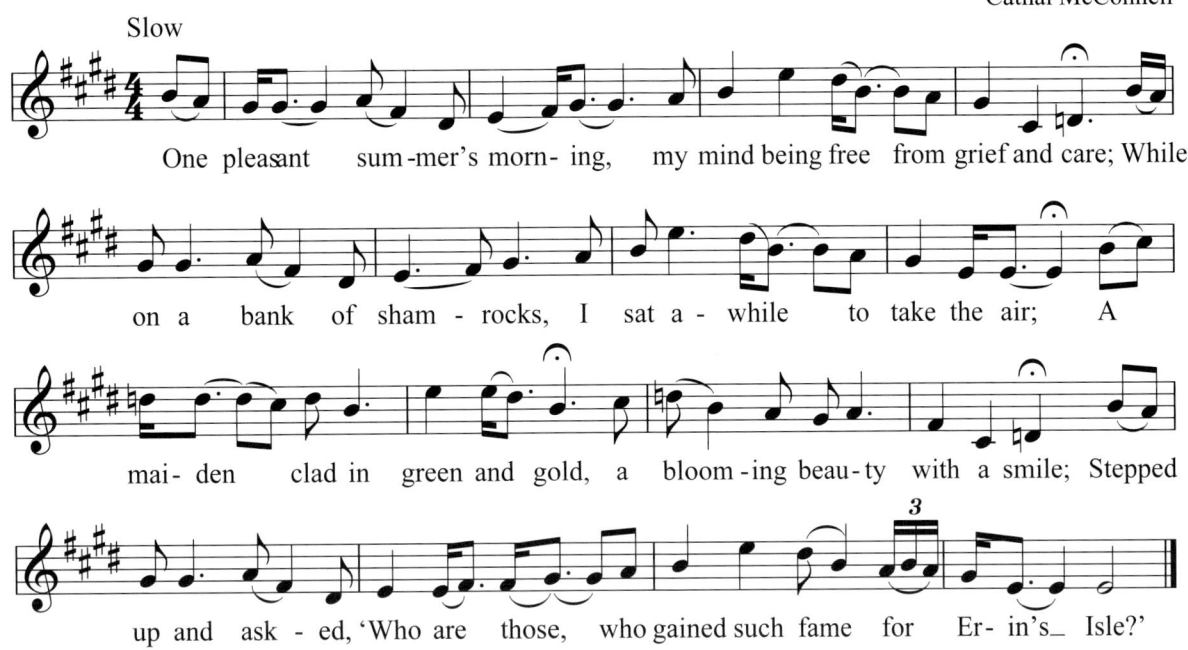

1. One pleasant summer's morning, my mind being free from grief and care,
    While on a bed of shamrocks, I sat awhile to take the air;
    A maiden clad in green and gold, a blooming beauty with a smile,
    Stepped up and asked me, 'Who are those, who gained such fame for Erin's Isle?'

2. I pondered in amazement, the question being a serious one,
    As I gazed upon her dancing eyes, that sparkled in the morning sun,
    'Are you the Maid of Erin?' 'I am,' she answered with a smile,
    'For I always love to hear of those Illustrious Sons of Erin's Isle.

3. 'Pray tell if you are able, who gained the day at Clontarf too,
    Who gained the day at Fontenoy, was he a son of Erin's too?
    When ruin and desolation, our fertile country over-ran,
    Who called emancipation, oh say was he an Irishman?'

4. 'It was a son of Erin's who gained the day at Clontarf too,
    A man of noble parentage, those ancient foes he did subdue;
    And were it not for Irishmen, the French would surely have to fly,
    For with brave Sarsfield by her side, they gained the day at Fontenoy.'

5. 'Think on those noble heroes, who have departed from our shore,
    Old Grattan, Burke and Davitt, Wolfe Tone, Lord Edward and Tom Moore,
    Young Emmet taken in his prime, the three Manchester Martyrs then,
    Young Allen, Larkin and O'Brien, three noble-hearted Irishmen.'

To last 2 lines of tune:

'Oh Madam, pay attention, for if you'll only wait awhile,
I mean to tell you plainly, who gained such fame for Erin's Isle.'

Cathal McConnell learned this song from Hugh Lee of Aughakillymaude in 1962. It is a rare song, but with similarities to Peter Flanagan's *Green Robed Inisfail*.

In Praise of John Magee

John Maguire

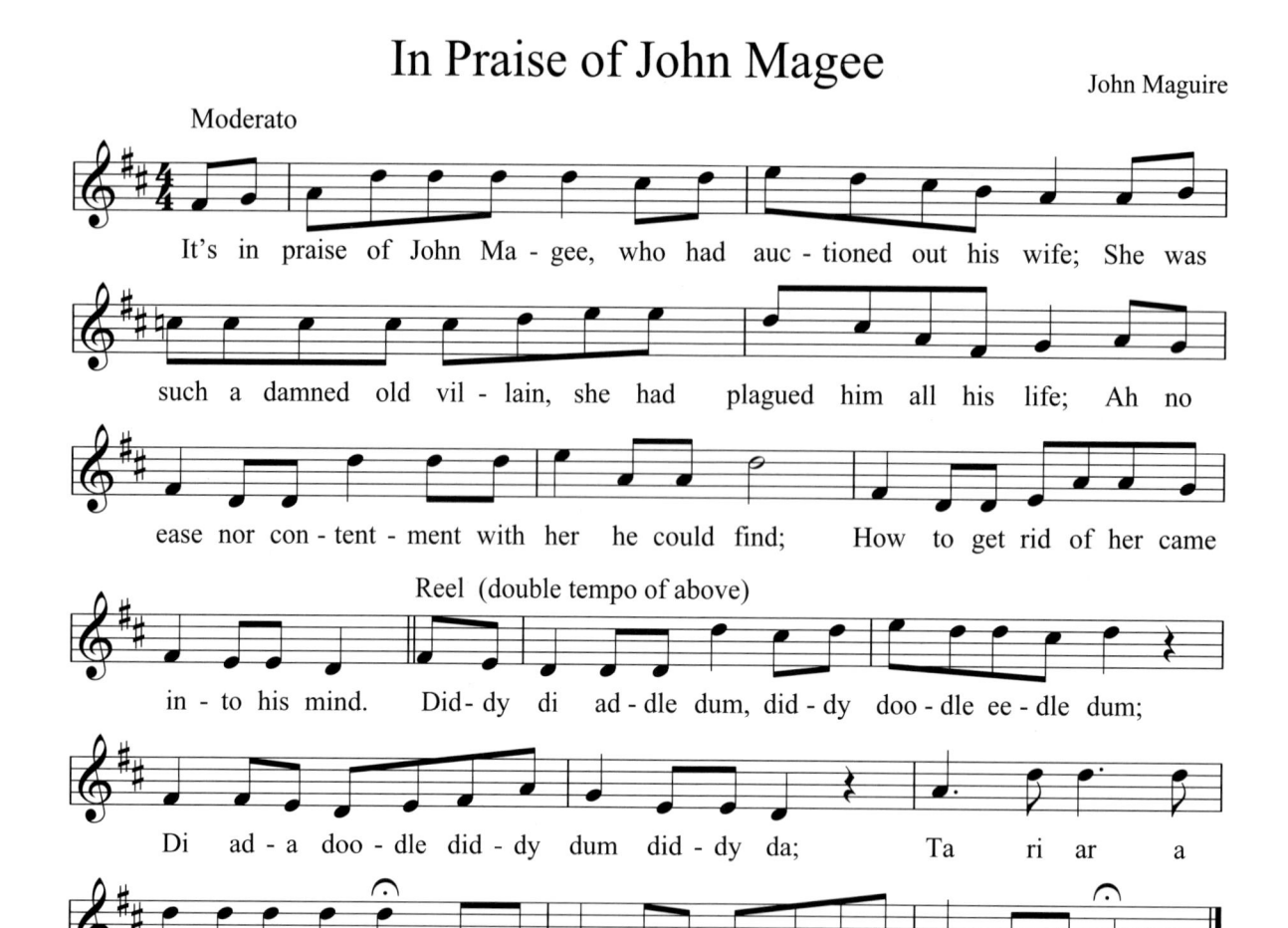

1. It's in praise of John Magee, who had auctioned out his wife,
   She was such a damned old villain, she had plagued him all his life;
   Ah no peace nor contentment with her he could find;
   How to get rid of her, came into his mind.
   REFRAIN - lilted in Reel tempo

2. When the chimney-sweeper's wife heard the auctioneer roar,
   With a stone in her stocking, she gave him a blow;
   He up with his crutch and knocked this woman down,
   The sweep with the broom came crack upon her crown.
   REFRAIN - lilted in Reel tempo

3. The first that came up was a jolly roving tar,
   And he on his way from the Indian war;
   He waited till he heard the auctioneer roar;
   No matter what the bidding, he'd bid a shilling more.
   REFRAIN - lilted in Reel tempo

4. Oh a jobber from Killarney, for the auction he did wait,
   With his mouth wide open like a Newton gate;
   Oh he took a look upon and he said that she would do,
   'She's a damn nice figure and well-rigged too.'
   REFRAIN - lilted in Reel tempo

5. Well the next that came up was a farmer riding by,
   He bought this old woman, aye at shillings twenty-five;
   Now he bein' a widower and a friend of her own
   He stuck her up behind him and they both drove home.
   REFRAIN – lilted in Reel tempo

6. It's now for to finish and end all my strife;
   John Magee has got home but he hasn't got a wife;
   'Well the devil run along with him,' the auctioneer did say,
   And, 'Amen,' said the women, 'sure we'll all buy away.'

This comic song is from John Maguire of Roslea, recorded by Robin Morton in 1971. John Maguire got the song from a neighbour, Patrick Caddin, who may have composed this song. In *Come Day, Go Day, God Send Sunday,* Robin Morton says that the practice of selling one's wife existed in England up to the last quarter of the 19th century. This practice was the basis for Thomas Hardy's novel, *The Mayor of Casterbridge,* written in 1886. There were, however, some saving graces for the woman. Sometimes the woman sold her husband and sometimes the woman was sold to her lover, formalising an existing situation so that all parties could save face in a time when divorce was unavailable to the common people. This song seems to refer to the latter practice as suggested by, 'Now he bein' a widower and a friend of her own.'

Interestingly, the tune used for this song, which is also lilted as a reel at the end of each verse, is that used for the bawdy song *The Cuckoo's Nest*, also commonly played as a hornpipe and reel.

Kate from Ballinamore

Annie McKenzie

1. Sure when I was young and fond of fun, like all young dashing blades;
   It was my delight both day and night, to court a handsome maid;
   With her I'd walk, with her I'd talk, like thousands done before;
   It was little I knew she'd prove untrue, young Kate from Ballinamore.

2. It's her father Frank that I must thank, for bein' in this state;
   Although I was poor I couldn't endure, to court his daughter Kate;
   I went to Kate for to relate, her solace to implore;
   Ah, what'll I do but follow you, young Kate from Ballinamore.

3. Says she, 'My dearest dear, I'd like to be a soldier's bride,
   Like a true and faithful comrade, fighting by your side.'
   So I went away without delay, and joined the Forty-Four;
   So now today I'm miles away, from Kate from Ballinamore.

4. Well it being six months after, a letter I received;
   I thought it was for comfort, but my poor heart it was grieved;
   The first few lines that I read, it was cruel o'er and o'er;
   She was goin' to get wed to a farmer's son, that came round Ballinamore.

5. So come all ye young and dashing lads, a warning take from me;
   And don't put too much confidence, in any wee lass you see;
   They'll tell you this and they'll tell you that, and they'll do as they done before;
   They'll curl their hair and they'll leave you there, like Kate from Ballinamore.

Annie McKenzie learned this song from Malachy Quirk in Swanlinbar in the 1960s.

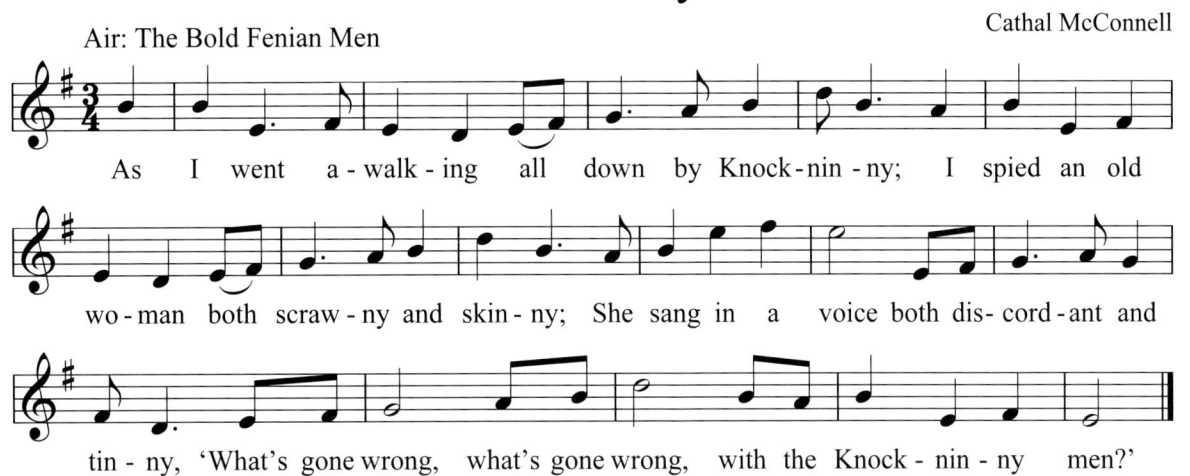

The Knockninny Men

Air: The Bold Fenian Men

Cathal McConnell

As I went a-walking all down by Knock-nin-ny; I spied an old wo-man both scraw-ny and skin-ny; She sang in a voice both dis-cord-ant and tin-ny, 'What's gone wrong, what's gone wrong, with the Knock-nin-ny men?'

1. As I went a-walking all down by Knockninny,
   I spied an old woman both scrawny and skinny,
   She sang in a voice both discordant and tinny,
   'What's gone wrong, what's gone wrong, with the Knockninny men?

2. 'Sure their footballers do badly, they lose all their matches,
   They're awful bad kicks and they're even worse catches,
   And the Balenaleck boys can run through them in batches,
   What's gone wrong, what's gone wrong, with the Knockninny men?

3. 'Sean ...., that villian, he's got them all running,
   With his big motorcar and his minibus humming,
   And they don't know a damn if they're going or coming,
   What's gone wrong, what's gone wrong, with the Knockninny men?

4. As she rounded the corner she said, 'Why should I tarry,
   Sure the boys around here, sure they're all like ....,
   They'll love you and leave you but they're damned slow to marry,
   What's gone wrong, what's gone wrong, with the Knockninny men?'

Another comic song from Sandy McConnell, Cathal's father, bewailing the state of the local men.

Lough Erne's Shore

Cathal McConnell

1. One morning as I went a-fowling, bright Phoebus adorn-ed the plain;
   'Twas down by the shores of Lough Erne, I met with a beautiful dame;
   Her voice was so sweet and so pleasing, with beautiful notes she did sing;
   Oh the innocent fowl of the forest, their love unto her they did bring.

2. Oh it bein' the first time that I met her, my heart it did jump with surprise,
   I thought that she could be no mortal, but an angel that fell from the skies;
   Her hair it resembled gold tresses, her skin was as white as the snow,
   And her cheeks were as red as the roses, that bloom around Lough Erne's shore.

3. When I found out that my love was was eloping, these words unto her I did say,
   'Oh take me to your habitation, since Cupid has led me astray;
   Oh had I the lamp of Aladdin, his rings and his jewels and more,
   I would part with them all to gain you, and live around Lough Erne's shore.'

Lovely Jane from Enniskea

John Maguire

1. One evening fair in lovely June, I carelessly did stray;
   The fields with acclamation rang, and flowers decked each vale;
   Fair and delightful was the scene, and one thing seemed more gay,
   And that was Jane that's free from stain, in lovely Enniskea.

2. The demesne walls I thus ascend and thus accosted Jane;
   Said I, 'Fair maid pray condescend and heal your lovesick swain,
   For I am deep in love with you, rely on what I say,
   Oh do not chide, but be my bride, fair Jane of Enniskea.'

3. 'Indeed young man I know you not, although you have my name;
   It must have been that man told you, goes down by yonder stream.
   It is no use, I loved a youth, and single I will stay;
   A maid I'll roam till he comes home through lovely Enniskea.'

4. 'Oh it was that man goes by yon stream, told me your name was Jane,
   But from what you state I plainly see your favour I won't gain;
   Come tell to me the lad you loved, and then I'll go away.'
   'Ah the truth to tell he's Willie Bell, that strayed from Enniskea.'

5. These last words took me by surprise, indeed I was the man,
   That led me at once to know my charming Jane McCann,
   The token was a golden ring, she gave when going away,
   That I showed to Jane to prove her swain in lovely Enniskea.

6. When she saw the mark upon the ring, she clasped her arms round me,
   'Oh Willie dear, it's ten long years since last I did you see;
   You're welcome quite, my heart's delight, home from Americay,
   Until your Jane that's free from stain in lovely Enniskea.'

7. Then slowly we did travel, down by yon flowery vale,
   Till we reached her mama's cottage, lay near to Ravensvale;
   We quickly published up our banns, got married without delay,
   Me and my love were like two doves in lovely Enniskea.

Robin Morton recorded John Maguire singing this song in 1971. Robin regarded John not only as a source for tunes, but as an important collecter himself. John learned this song from his mother, who was also an acclaimed singer. Enniskea is between the border and Dundalk. See also *In Praise Of John Magee, The Maid Of Magheracloon, Tom Kelly's Cow, Willie's Ghost* and *Erin The Green*.

The Maid of the Colehill

John Maguire

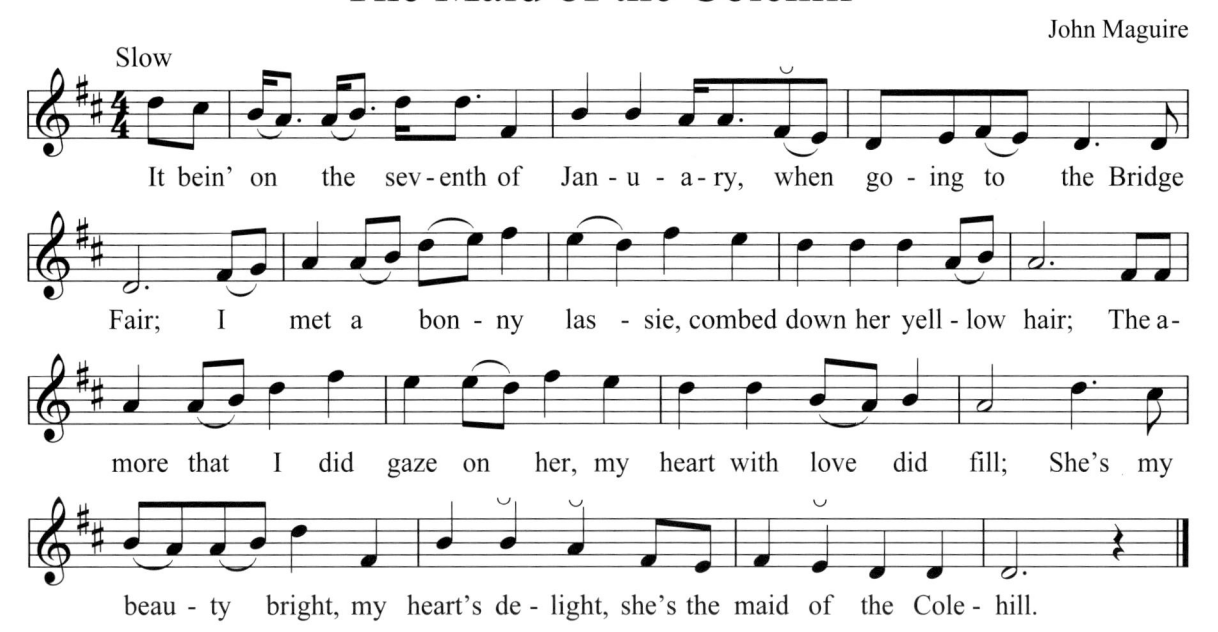

1. It bein' on the seventh of January, when going to the Bridge Fair,
   I met a bonny lassie, combed down her yellow hair;
   The more that I did gaze on her, my heart with love did fill;
   She's my beauty bright, my heart's delight, she's the maid of the Colehill.

2. I had no mind to tarry long when I left home that day;
   I had no mind to tarry long when I left Lisnaskea;
   But meeting with some friends of mine when I arriv-ed there,
   So kindly they saluted me and said, 'You're welcome to the Fair.'

3. We then went into a public house, where there we all sat down;
   The jugs of punch came tumbling and the toast went merrily round;
   The liquor it was plenty and we drank with a free good-will;
   Here's a flowing glass to the blooming lass, she's the maid of the Colehill.

4. Some people please to tell me that my love she does me slight,
   But when I'm in her company, I think all things are right;
   She says herself she'll marry me, and that with a free good-will;
   She'll forsake her friends and relations, and likewise the Colehill.

Robin Morton collected this from John Maguire of Rosslea in 1971, who in turn had collected it from his friend and neighbour, Paddy McMahon, brother of flute player James McMahon, who features in the tunes' section. This was Paddy's favourite song. All the places mentioned are in the vicinity of Enniskillen. "Bridge" is probably Maguiresbridge and Colehill is now a housing estate on the edge of Enniskillen.

My Charming Edward Boyle

John Maguire

1. Oh you tender hearted maidens, of a high and a low degree,
   Likewise you wounded lovers, come sympathise with me;
   For here I am bewailing a young man I adore;
   He's now fled from my arms, bound for Colombia's shore.

2. In the county of Fermanagh, in the parish of Roslea,
   In the townland of Grahwarren, near the mountains of Slievebeagh;
   He was reared by honest parents, and of St Patrick's soil,
   But now they're sunk in sorrow for the loss of Edward Boyle.

3. Right well I do remember all in the month of May,
   When Flora's flowery mantle decked the meadows gay,
   When every thing seemed charming and blooms too on her smile;
   I parted with my own true love, my charming Edward Boyle.

4. 'Twas on a Monday morning his friends did him convey,
   All from the town of Dundalk, from that round to the quay;
   With courage bold he did set sail and left the shamrock shore;
   May all joys be with you Edward, will I ever see you more?

5. He was the pride of Collegelands, so well his flute could play;
   And the country is all lonesome, since our Edward went away;
   His comrades all, both great and small, you'd swear they'd leave their soil,
   In hopes once more on Colombia's shore, for one sight of young Edward Boyle.

Collected by Robin Morton from the singing of John Maguire. This song is also from the Roslea area.

The Roslea Farewell

Gabriel McArdle

1. One night as I lay slumbering, in my silent dreams at home;
   Some rakish thoughts came into my mind, which caused me for to roam;
   To leave my native counterey, and the girl that I adore;
   Sure I thought then to take a trip, and leave my home once more.

2. At the leaving of the town, brave boys, and passing the Barracks Hill;
   'Twas there I seen my own wee girl, and her eyes with tears did fill;
   I embraced her in my arms, and I gave her kisses nine;
   Sayin', 'If ever I return again, fair maid you will be mine.'

3. 'Oh John, dear John, my darling John, what makes you go away?
   Oh stay at home and do not roam, from the green fields of Roslea;
   My wages I would freely give, when my term-time is o'er;
   If you'll agree and stay with me, and leave your home no more.'

4. 'Oh Mary, my lovely Mary, my ship lies in Belfast;
   Tomorrow morning it will sail, and you and I must part;
   Tomorrow morning it will sail, straight away from Erin's shore.'
   And without delay John sailed next day, far from his home once more.

5. When John he arrived in Glasgow, the boys all gathered around;
   Saying, 'You may go home, Roslea brave boy, for the harvest it's cut down;
   You may go home, Roslea brave boy, straight back to Ireland's shore.'
   And straight away John sailed next day, back to his land once more.

6. When Mary she saw that John was home, her heart it filled with joy;
   Saying, 'You're welcome back into my arms, you're my own and pride and joy;
   You're welcome into my arms, for you and I've loved long;
   And let them say whate'er they may, our courtship will go on.'

7. Where the trout and salmon they leap upon, down by Lough Erne's bay;
   There John led Mary by the hand, to the Chapel in Roslea;
   The lark and linnet they trilled their notes, they trilled them o'er and o'er;
   As John got wed to his Mary, and he left his home no more.

Gabriel learned this song from an old reel-to-reel recording made by Maura McConnell of Mrs McEntee of Emyvale, County Monaghan. A singing friend of Gabriel's, Geordie Hanna of Tyrone, sings a version called *Brockage Brae.*

The Rushes Green

Cathal McConnell

As I went out one morning, to view the fields and forest green; With my two hunting beagles, in order there some game to see; There I saw none but Mary, she appeared to me like a virgin queen; She was at her daily labour, and a-reaping of her rushes green.

1. As I went out one morning to view the fields and forest green,
   With my two hunting beagles, in order there some game to see;
   There I saw none but Mary, she appeared to me like a virgin queen;
   She was at her daily labour, and a-reaping of her rushes green.

2. As I looked all around me, to see what persons I might see,
   There I saw none but my Mary, whom I embraced most tenderly;
   She said, 'Young man go easy, oh go your way and let me be,
   Don't toss my rushes carelessly, hard labour I have gained by thee.'

3. 'If I tossed your rushes carelessly, a greener bunch I'll reap for you,
   So sit you down beside me and a pleasant story I'll tell you.'
   'It's hard, kind sir, to refuse you, although your false love has led me astray,
   So I'll sit down beside you, 'till the morning dew does fade away.'

4. As my love and I sat courting, beneath yon greenwood laurel tree,
   The small birds sang melodiously, changing their notes from tree to tree;
   The lark she joined in chorus, as I embraced my virgin queen;
   For Mary, my love Mary, and her bonny bunch of rushes green.

5. As my love and I got married, great riches she has gained by me,
   She has servants for to wait on her and save her from all slavery;
   Her waist so small and slender, the whole world I would range it round,
   For Mary, my love Mary, and her bonny bunch of rushes brown.

Another song from the repertoire of Katie Gunn.

The Second-Hand Trousers I Bought in Belcoo

Cathal and Mickey McConnell

1. There are stories afloat that are hard to believe;
   There are stories afloat that are meant to deceive;
   But here is a story that's perfectly true,
   'Bout the second-hand trousers I bought in Belcoo.
   CHORUS: Tra la la (Tra la la);
              Tra la loo (Tra la loo);
   'Bout the second-hand trousers I bought in Belcoo.

2. Now the missus was sick, I give Jimmy the job;
   And when he was leaving, I'd give him ten bob;
   He bought me these yokers and he hoped they would do;
   They're a fair pack of .... up there in Belcoo.

3. When the wife saw the trousers, she flew in a rage;
   Sayin', 'They're no wear at all, for a man of your age;
   With one leg so black and the other so blue,
   Ah they'd rob a child's bottle up there in Belcoo.'

4. Well I raced from the kitchen out into the yard;
   When me own dog he saw me, he nearly went mad;
   The hens flew like blazes, the ould rooster crew,
   At the second-hand trousers I bought in Belcoo.

5. Well that evening two ladies arrived in a car;
   They said, 'We're collecting for the Arney Bazaar.'
   I give them a parcel and they said, 'Thank you.'
   'Twas the second-hand trousers I bought in Belcoo.

6. Well at the Bazaar, shure we all had great fun,
   When the trousers went up and the rickety spun;
   In the mad tear for tickets I only got two,
   But I won back the trousers I got in Belcoo.

This song was written by Sandy McConnell and is sung by Cathal and Mickey McConnell on the accompanying CD. It is sometimes also sung as *The Orangeman's Trousers*. The "rickety" was the revolving wheel for selecting the winning number.

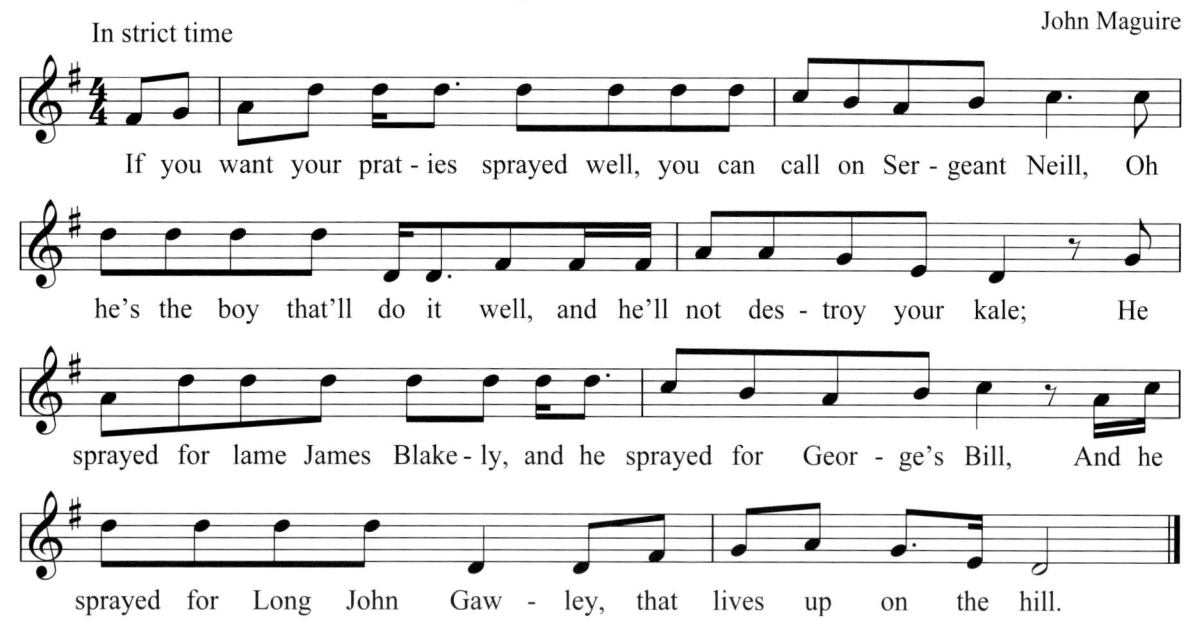

Sergeant Neill

John Maguire

In strict time

[musical notation]

If you want your prat-ies sprayed well, you can call on Ser-geant Neill, Oh he's the boy that'll do it well, and he'll not des-troy your kale; He sprayed for lame James Blake-ly, and he sprayed for Geor-ge's Bill, And he sprayed for Long John Gaw-ley, that lives up on the hill.

1. If you want your praties sprayed well, you can call on Sergeant Neill,
   Oh he's the boy that'll do it well, and he'll not destroy your kale;
   He sprayed for lame James Blakely, and he sprayed for George's Bill,
   And he sprayed for Long John Gawley, that lives upon the hill.

2. He sprayed for Peter Lowry and he sprayed for Larry's Hugh,
   And he turned to Greaghollia and he sprayed for Bishop Grew;
   He sprayed for Patrick Anthony, and for the Widow's Pat,
   And he sprayed for John The Carpenter, that wore the three-cocked hat.

3. He sprayed for the McGrory's, that lived up at the Road,
   And he sprayed for Paddy Berry, that lives in Mullin's Cove,
   He sprayed for Tommy Armstrong, that kept the kicking mule,
   And he sprayed for decent Robert Ellett, that hopped round on the stool.

From John Maguire of Roslea and included by Robin Morton in *Come Day, Go Day, God Send Sunday.*

Sweet William's Ghost

Cathal McConnell

Lady Margaret she lay on her fine feather bed; The midnight hour drew near; When a ghostly form came to her bed, and to her did appear, appear; and to her did appear.

1. Lady Margaret she lay on her fine feather bed,
   The midnight hour drew near;
   When a ghostly form came to her bed,
   And to her did appear, appear,
   And to her did appear.

2. 'Are you my father the King then?' she cried,
   'Or are you my brother John,
   Or are you my true love William,
   Coming home from Scotland along, along,
   Coming home from Scotland along?'

3. 'No I'm not your father the King then,' he cried,
   'Nor am I your brother John,
   But I'm your true love William,
   Coming home from Scotland along, along,
   Coming home from Scotland along.'

4. 'Oh Margaret, Lady Margaret,' he cried,
   'For love or charity
   Will you give me back the plighted troth,
   That once love I gave thee, gave thee,
   That once love I gave thee.'

5. 'No I'll not give you back the plighted troth,
   Or any such a thing,
   Until you take me to my own father's hall
   Where oft-times we have been, have been,
   Where oft-times we have been.'

6. So he took her to her own father's hall
   And as they entered in,
   The gates blew open of their own free will
   For to let young William in, in,
   For to let young William in.

7. 'Oh Margaret, Lady Margaret,' he cried,
   'For love or charity,
   Will you give me back the plighted troth,
   That once love I gave thee, gave thee,
   That once love I gave thee.'

8. 'I'll not give you back the plighted troth,
   Nor any such a thing,
   Until you bring me to yon high churchyard,
   And there marry me with a ring, a ring,
   And there marry me with a ring.'

9. So he took her to yon high churchyard,
   And as they entered in,
   The gates flew open of their own free will
   To let young William in, in,
   To let young William in.

10. 'Oh Margaret, Lady Margaret,' he cried,
    For love or charity,
    Will you give me back the plighted troth
    That once love I gave thee, gave thee,
    That once love I gave thee.'

11. Then out of her pocket she drew then a cross
    And she placed it on his breast,
    Saying; 'Here is back your plighted troth,
    And in heaven your soul find rest, find rest,
    And in heaven your soul find rest.'

12. 'Oh the wind doth blow and the moorcocks crow,
    And it's almost breaking day,
    And it's time that the living should depart from the dead,
    So my darling I must away, away,
    So my darling I must away.'

Cathal McConnell learned Sweet William's Ghost from his father, Sandy. It is an almost complete version of the ancient ballad, No. 77, in Child's listing.

Tom Kelly's Cow

John Maguire

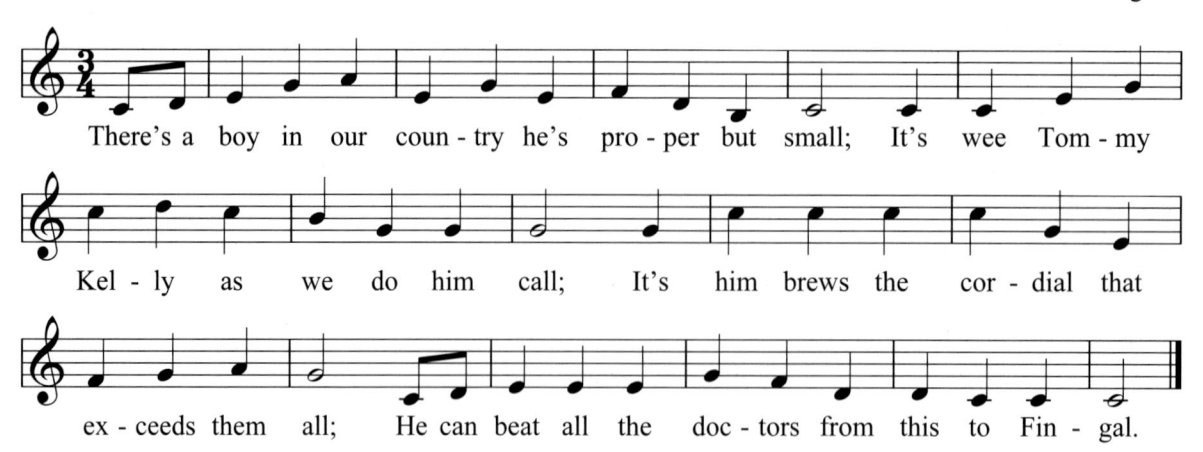

1. There's a boy in our country, he's proper but small,
   It's wee Tommy Kelly, as we do him call;
   It's him brews the cordial that exceeds them all;
   He can beat all the doctors from this to Fingal.

2. If you were sick and was ready to die,
   One glass of Tom's poteen would raise your heart high;
   You could heave it up higher and nearer your nose;
   It's an Irishman's toast then wherever he goes.

3. When the cow took a notion this drink for to take;
   She pulled and she pulled till she pulled out her stake;
   She got to the barrel and she drank her fill,
   'Oh be jeepers,' says Tom, 'she's left none for the still.'

4. Next morning she woke with a sad broken horn,
   Cursing the day and the hour she was born;
   She cursed Tom and John, Mr Beattie likewise,
   And all the still-tinkers that's under the skies.

5. Oh the cow came to Tom and she whispered in his ear,
   'You won't tell John that I got on the beer;
   If you don't, 'pon my honour with a heart and a half,
   I will bring you against Lammas a fine heifer calf.'

Another song collected by Robin Morton from John Maguire of Rosslea. This song features yet another rogue cow (see *Ballyconnell Fair,* page 57). John learned this song while still at school from Mrs Boyle, a first cousin of Tom Kelly, who was then still living.

The Town of Swanlinbar

Cathal McConnell

Oh, early one morning John with his spirits high; Oh it's
John, dearest John you are a good boy; Oh it's
John, dearest John you are a good boy But I
like to see you working late and ear - ly

1. Oh early one morning, John with his spirits high;
   Oh it's John, dearest John, you are a good boy;
   Oh it's John, dearest John, you are a good boy;
   But I like to see you working late and early.

2. Oh John began a rushing and preparing for the fair;
   Oh it's John, dearest John, are you going anywhere?
   I'm not going very far, to the town of Swanlinbar,
   I'll be back between eight and early morning.

3. Have you money in your pocket to give to me to spend?
   I've money in my pocket but none of it to lend;
   I've got money in my pocket but none of it for John;
   For I need you working early in the morning.

4. In sport to fight and scold with you is a thing I never do;
   You know I never mean it when I'm arguing with you;
   So here is ten shillings, you can have it now dear John;
   But I need you working early in the morning.

5. Throw your mantle o'er your shoulder and come along with John;
   We'll have a glass of whiskey and a verse of a song;
   If your money it runs out you can call about on John,
   And we'll go home drunk as Baltic in the morning

6. Now, whiskey is a cordial I do not like at all,
   Since the Landlady's measure has got so very small;
   A pint of good porter will satisfy us all,
   And we'll go home in good humour in the morning.

7. It's now that I've got married and a wife for to keep;
   A babe in the cradle and a babe to put to sleep;
   It's the outside of the door I'm scarce allowed to creep;
   That's the life of a married man this morning.

Cathal McConnell had this song from John and Valerie McManus. It is another song from the large repretoire of John's mother, Katie Gunn. Like Sandy McConnell's *Ballyconnell Fair*, the song is based on real people. Swanlinbar is pronounced "Swadlinbar" and is locally referred to as "Swad".

The Wee Weaver

from Paddy Tunney

Freely

I am a wee wea-ver, con-fined to my loom; My love she's as fair as the red rose in June; She is loved by all oth-ers and that does grieve me; My heart's in the bos-om of love-ly Ma-ry.

1. I am a wee weaver, confined to my loom
   My love she's as fair as the red rose in June
   She is loved by all others and that does grieve me
   My heart's in the bosom of lovely Mary

2. As Mary and Willie roamed by yonder green bower
   Where Mary and Willie spent many a happy hour
   Where the thrush and the linnet do consort in chore
   To sing the praises of Mary round Lough Erne Shore

3. As Mary and Willie roamed by yonder lough side
   Said Willie to Mary, 'Will you be my bride?'
   So this couple got married and they'll roam no more
   They'll have pleasures and treasures round Lough Erne Shore

Willie Rambler

Gabriel McArdle

1. When I was young and in my prime, at the age of twenty-four;
   I left Lough Erne's lovely banks, to England I sailed o'er;
   'Twas there I spied a maiden fair, of honour and renown;
   'Twas of her I did ask the way, to famous London town.

2. 'Young man, are you a stranger, were you never here before?
   Come tell to me from where you came, unto this country o'er.'
   I said, 'I am an Irish lad, who lately has sailed o'er,
   And they call me Willie Rambler, from sweet Lough Erne's shore.'

3. 'If you be Willie Rambler,' this charming maid did say,
   'What would you take if you'd consent, and with me come away?'
   'Five hundred pounds a year I'd take.' 'I'd give you that and more,
   And I'd crown you Willie Rambler, from sweet Lough Erne's shore.'

4. Were you ever on Lough Erne's banks, on a pleasant summer's day?
   When the blackbird and thrush, in ev'ry bush, they charm their notes so gay;
   And the fame of Ballyshannon town by far exceeds them all;
   From June, July and August, when the salmon leaps the fall.

TO LAST 2 LINES OF TUNE:

From green Clyhore, to Ely Lodge, a spot of high renown;
Where the small birds sing out their chorus round you, lovely Castletown.

Gabriel McArdle heard this song around 1975 from musician Mick Hoy from Derrygonnelly. It was also sung by Ben McGrath and others in the area. Gabriel's rendition of this song can be found on the CD "Dog Big and Dog Little", ceirníní cladaigh, cc51CD.

BIBLIOGRAPHY

Allingham, William. *An essay reprinted from Household Words to which Allingham contributed it without a signature on Jan. 10, 1852 (No. 94)*. Ceol, vol. 111, No.1.

Boys of the Lough, The. *Music and Song from the Boys of the Lough.* Gilderoy Music 1977.

Breathnach, Breandan. *Irish Folk Music Studies, Vol. 2, 1974–75:* Essay on Piper Jackson, pp. 41–57.

Breathnach, Breandan *Ceol Rince na hÉireann, Cuid 1*, 1963; *Cuid 2*, 1976; *Cuid 3*, 1985; *Cuid 4*, 1996; *Cuid 5*, 1999.

Breathnach, Breandan. *Folk Music and Dances of Ireland.* Mercier Press, Cork, 1971.

Bunting, Edward. *The Ancient Music of Ireland.* Walton's Galleries, Dublin, 1969. First published 1796. Reprinted 1809 and 1840.

Burns, Padraic. *The Ulster Singer.* Printed at *The Fermanagh Times* Office

Carleton, William. *The Autobiography.* First Published 1896. White Row Press, 1996.

A Journal of Irish Music. vol. 111, No. 1.

Corcoran, Sean. *Songs, Music and Stories of an Ulster Community.* Collected and edited by Sean Corcoran, 1986.

Dick, James C. *The Songs of Robert Burns.* Folklore Associates, Pennsylvania, 1962. First published 1903.

Feldman, Allen and O'Doherty, Eamon. *The Northern Fiddler.* Blackstaff Press, Belfast, 1979.

Galvin, Patrick. *Irish Song of Resistance.* Oak Publications, 1962.

Glassie, Henry. *All Silver and no Brass; An Irish Christmas Mumming.* Indiana University Press, 1975.

Glassie, Henry. *Passing the Time in Ballymenone: Folklore and History of an Ulster Community.* O'Brien Press, Dublin, 1982.

Gow, Neil. *The Beauties of Neil Gow.* Celtic Music, 1983. First published 1819.

Hanvey, Bobbie. *Merely Players: Portraits from Northern Ireland.* Colourpoint Books, 1999.

Healy, James N. *The Second Book of Irish Ballads.* Mercier, 1962.

Henry, Sam. *Songs of the People.* University of Georgia Press, 1990. First publications 1923–39 by *The Northern Constitution*, Coleraine, Northern Ireland.

Kerr, James S. *Kerr's Collection of Merry Melodies for the Violin.* Kerr's, Glasgow, 1875.

Kennedy, Peter, ed. *Folksongs of Britain and Ireland.* Cassell and Company Ltd, 1975.

MacDonald, Keith Norman. *The Skye Collection*. Cranford Publications, 1979. First published 1887.

Magennis, Peter. *The Ribbon Informer*. Frederick Bell and Co, London, 1874.

Magennis, Peter. *Poems of Peter Magennis*. Printed at *The Fermanagh Times* office, September 1887.

Maguire, Sean & Keegan, Josephine. *Irish Tunes by the 100, Vol. 1*. Celtic Music, 1975.

Milligan Fox, Charlotte. *Annals of the Irish Harpers*. London, John 1917 (Includes *Memoirs of Arthur O'Neill,* pp. 137–200).

Moloney, Colette. *The Irish Music Manuscripts of Edward Bunting* (1773–1843). Published by Irish Traditional Music Archive, 63 Merrion Square, Dublin, 2000.

Morton, Robin. *Come Day, Go Day, God Send Sunday*. Routledge and Kegan Paul Ltd, 1973.

McCusker, Breege. *Journal of the Clogher Historical Society, 1988*.

O'Canainn, Tomas. *Traditional Music of Ireland,* Ossian. Originally published by Routledge and Kegan Paul Ltd. 1978.

O'Lochlainn, Colm. *Irish Street Ballads* and *More Irish Street Ballads,* Pan Books, 1978. First published Dublin 1939.

O'Neill, Captain Francis. *The Dance Music of Ireland, 1,001 Gems*. Walton's Galleries, Dublin. First Published 1907.

O'Neill, Captain Francis. *O'Neill's Music of Ireland*. Published by Daniel Michel Collins, New York. First published 1903.

O'Neill, Captain Francis. *Irish Minstrels and Musicians*. Mercier Press, 1987. First published 1913.

O'Neill, Captain Francis. *Waifs and Strays of Gaelic Melody*. Mercier Press. First published 1922.

Ryan, William Bradbury. *Ryan's Mammoth Collection*. Mel Bay, 1995. First published 1883.

Skinner, J Scott. *The Scottish Violinist*. Bayley and Ferguson, Glasgow.

Tunney, Paddy. *The Stone Fiddle*. Gilbert Dalton Ltd, Dublin, 1979.

Tunney, Paddy. *Where songs do Thunder: Travels in Traditional Song*. Appletree Press, Belfast, 1991.

Index of Dance Tunes

Title	Type	Page
Aberdeen Lasses, The	reel	109
Banshee, The (McMahon's)	Reel	98
Big John's Hard Jig	Jig	72
Big John's Reel	Reel	84
Blackberry Blossom, The	Reel	90
Blackbird, The	Air, Hornpipe & Reel	128
Blue Ribbon, The	Highland	123
Bobby Treacy's Barn Dance	Barn dance	124
Bonny Boys of Ballintra	Reel	109
Boy in the Gap, The	Reel	92
Boys of 25, The	Reel	98
Braes of Auchintyre, The	Reel	110
Brown's Hornpipe	Hornpipe	116
Castlebar Reel, The	Reel	93
Chase her through the Garden	Reel	89
Chorus Jig, The	Reel	91
Cocktail, The	Reel	87
Collegians of Glasgow, The	Reel	110
Corratistune Rose, The	Air	120
Dickie Gossip	Reel	84
Drumshanbo Jig, The	Jig	80
Duke of Brunswick, The	Hornpipe	117
Eddie Duffy's Hornpipe	Hornpipe	114
Eddie's Lannigan's Ball	Jig	78
Eddie's Monaghan Twig	Reel	87
Ereshire Lasses, The	Reel	111
Fairy Waltz, The (Hugh Crawford's)	Waltz	125
Fermanagh Quickstep, The	Jig	123
Fisher's Hornpipe	Hornpipe	115
Girl in Danger, The	Reel	86
Glass of Beer, The	Reel	85
Grand Spy, The	Reel	111
Green Grow the Rashes	Highland	122
Greg's Pipes	Reel	112
Hand me Down the Tacklings	Reel	101
Handsome Sally	Reel	102
Hard Road to Travel, It's a	Reel	93
Hawk of Ballyshannon, The	Reel	86
Heart of my Kitty, The	Jig	73
Hetty's Wishes	Reel	112
High Geese in the Bog, The	Jig	81
Humours of Glen, The	Jig	73
Humours of Loughrea, The	Reel	113
Humours of Mackin, The	Reel	107
Humours of Swanlinbar, The	Reel	100
I Lost my Love and I Care Not	Jig	74
Ivory Flute, The	Jig	82
Jackson's Babby	Jig	75
Jackson's Couge in the Morning	Jig	75
Jackson's Dairymaid	Reel	99
Jackson's Dream	Jig	76
Jackson's Postchaise	Jig	74
James McMahon's Hornpipe	Hornpipe	115
James McMahon's Jig	Jig	82
Jig Away the Donkey	Reel	88
Jig Away the Donkey	Reel	89
Jimmy Duffy's Barn Dances	Barn dance	119
Katie's Lilt	March	121
Lady Anne Montgomery	Reel	100
Lady Gardener's Troop Reel	Reel	108
Lady Luebeck	Reel	103
Lamentation of the Dead Perch, The	Jig	83
Leyeer's Hornpipe	Hornpipe	117
Loon Lasses, The (The Noone Lasses)	Reel	101
Maho Snaps, The	Jig	81
Maid in the Cherry Tree, The	Reel	99
McCormack's	Jig	78
McHugh's Reel	Reel	96
Milltown Lasses, The	Reel	103
Miss Adam's Hornpipe	Hornpipe	118
Miss Lacey's Hornpipe	Hornpipe	118
Miss Weatherburn's Reel	Reel	107
Mist in the Meadow, The	Jig	79
Neil Gow's	Highland	121

Index of Dance Tunes

Neils Gowan's Second Wife	Reel	108
New Ships a-Sailing, The	Reel	97
O Squeeze your Thighs	Jig	77
O'Connell's	Reel	97
Opera Reel, The	Reel	102
Paddy McGurn's Hornpipe	Hornpipe	116
Paidin O'Rafferty	Jig	79
Peter Flanagan's Stony Steps	Reel	96
Poor Scholar, The	Reel	104
Primrose Girl, The	Reel	105
Rakes of Inverary, The	Reel	106
Reel of Bogie, The	Reel	95
Rights of Irish, The	Jig	76
Ryan's Rant	Reel	95
Sally Kelly's	Reel	104
Sandy McConnell's	Waltz	125
Sir Edward Gunn's Reel	Reel	105
Sprig of Stradone, The	Jig	72
Stormy Saturday, The	Reel	94
Strawberry Banks, The	Reel	106
Sunny Banks Highland	Highland	124
Swing Swang	Reel	94
Tenpenny Bit, The	Jig	80
Three Scones of Boxtie, The	Reel	88
Top of the Hill	Set Dance	83
Uncle Hugh's	Reel	85
Uncle Hugh's Polka	Polka	120
Untitled	Reel	92
Untitled Highland	Highland	122
Untitled Hornpipe	Hornpipe	114
Untitled Waltz	Waltz	124
Valetta Waltz, The	Waltz	126
Wedding of Mary, The	Air	126
Wedding of Molly, The	Air	127
Wise Maid, The (The Humours of Swanlinbar)	Reel	190

Index of Songs

Ballyconnell Fair	57
Banks of Kilrea, The	130
Banks of the Clyde, The	131
Bessie the Beauty of Rossinure Hill	133
Bloomin' Bright Star of Bellisle, The	135
Bonny Green Tree, The	137
Dominick Noone the Traitor	138
Dumb, Dumb, Dumb	139
Edward on Lough Erne's Shore	140
Erin the Green	141
Frog's Wedding, The	143
Green-Robed Inisfail	144
Groves of Boho, The	145
I Have Travelled this Country	146
Illustrious Sons of Erin's Isle, The	147
In Praise of John Magee	148
Kate from Ballinamore	150
Knockninny Men, The	151
Lough Erne's Shore	152
Lovely Jane from Enniskea	153
Maid of the Colehill, The	155
My Charming Edward Boyle	156
Pat Gunn's Boat	21
Roslea Farewell, The	157
Royal Blackbird, The	129
Rushes Green, The	159
Second-Hand Trousers I Bought in Belcoo, The	160
Sergeant Neill	161
Sweet William's Ghost	162
Tom Kelly's Cow	164
Town of Swanlinbar, The	165
Wee Weaver, The	166
Willie Rambler	167